HOW TO HAVE
YOUR CAKE AND EAT IT

AFFAIR!

H. CAMERON BARNES

metro

Published by Metro Publishing Ltd,
3, Bramber Court, 2 Bramber Road,
London W14 9PB, England

www.blake.co.uk

This edition published in paperback in 2005

ISBN 1 84358 145 0

British Library Cataloguing-in-Publication Data:

A catalogue record for this book is available from the British Library.

Design by www.envydesign.co.uk

Printed in Great Britain by CPD

1 3 5 7 9 10 8 6 4 2

Papers used by Metro Publishing are natural, recyclable products made from
wood grown in sustainable forests. The manufacturing processes conform to
the environmental regulations of the country of origin.

'I am having an affair. No, I never thought I would or even could. But here I am in a two-plus-year-long affair with a man who is twelve years my senior. It started out innocently enough. Just friends. Our children are the same age; we talked a lot about them. Both our marriages were unhappy at the time; we talked about that. One thing led to another and here we are. It's not a matter of "love," although we are extremely fond of one another and love one another as friends. It's not a matter of not loving our spouses; it's more of a matter of there being something between us that could never be between either of us and anyone else. I have a husband who I greatly admire, but there is something my lover has that my husband doesn't; it's not his fault. My lover's wife, from what I can tell, seems to be a sensual woman who loved her husband very much at one time. But *all marriages change and sometimes you can't make things better again.*

'We have dealt with a lot of things over the past few years, and it's not all about sex ... sick kids, sick spouses, changing jobs...tons of everyday things we share. But, when we are with one another, it's like raw, animal chemistry mixed with a genuine affection for one another that neither of us can fight; believe me, I've tried. Our spouses don't know and never will; we agreed to that years ago. We have and will hurt no one. We would never interfere with or hurt each other's life; there are boundaries we do not cross (getting too close to the other's family, for example) and we have an agreement that no one will ever know about us. We have the best of all worlds: happy home lives and wonderful little interludes with one another.'

— Leigh, married fifteen years, one child

DEDICATION

To Former U.S. President William Jefferson Clinton

S ir, I wish you had been able to read the advice in Chapter 9. Knowing as well as anybody that D.C. is full of bright, beautiful, sexy and ambitious female lawyers, what you would have concluded is that the person who would have been the best companion for your affair was a thirty-ish attorney on the staff of the Democratic National Committee who specialised in election compliance law. She could have gone with you to every fund-raiser, stayed in a hotel room on the same floor, met with you at all hours and no one would have batted an eye! Not only would she have been the model of discretion, but she also probably would have been able to help you keep Al Gore out of trouble with all those questionable campaign contributions and freed you up so that you could have gone out campaigning and made his election a slam-dunk instead of putting him on the losing side of the most notorious case in electoral college history and ...

Who am I kidding? You wouldn't have listened, anyway. Look at you: while only a presidential candidate you told the world on national television that you had learned your lesson. Yet, in the midst of that embarrassing Paula Jones litigation, a thong-flash by a plump 22-year-old short-circuited your logic board. Your Place In History, always a big issue for you, is now assured, but it won't be quite the legacy that you would have preferred. My condolences.

No, this book is really dedicated to R. I will always have a grateful heart.

FOREWORD

ARE YOU OUT OF YOUR MIND? Here you are, standing alone in the psychology section of Waterstones, obviously reading this with great interest. What are you going to say when your neighbour, kid in tow, ambles over from the children's book section? Nothing comes to mind, does it? How long would it be before word got back to your spouse that you were thumbing through this? Three days? One day? As soon as your neighbour can get to the phone? Face it: We're talking dangerous stuff here.

Walk this over to History or, better yet, Computers. If you see someone out of the corner of your eye, shake your head slightly in bewilderment, shelve this book and pick up another.

OK. Have you thought of how you're going to pay for this book? Unless you buy at least half a dozen books a month from this particular shop, a credit card is out of the question.

Spouse: I see you were at Waterstones last month. Did you get that new John Grisham novel and hide it from me so that you could read it yourself first?

You: Duh.

You should probably purchase this from a shop that isn't somewhere you know the salespeople or where anyone in your community would normally go. Pay cash. And, while you're at it, buy a hardback copy of a book of approximately the same size, so that you can put on a different book jacket. Choose a book that everyone, including you, has already read, so it will look like you're behind the times and no one will ask what you're reading, if it's good, etc.; something like I'm OK, You're OK. Don't just steal a book cover off another book. It's criminal, and you're going to have more than your share of moral and ethical issues to face without considering your relationship to the bookshop or the local magistrate. Furthermore, since you're thinking of taking a dangerous voyage, this is not, psychologically, a good time to cut corners.

Oh, you're not in a bookshop right now? Think you're safely cruising the Internet? Do you have tracking recognition and removal software in place and activated? You don't want to be leaving footprints all over cyberspace, do you? Obviously, you're also not going to be able to physically pick up this book, go to the register and pay cash, either.

Spouse: You got a package from Amazon today. Mind if I open it?

You: Duh.

If you lack a safe delivery address, you'll need to have either a P.O. Box and you'll need to learn to use postal orders –

something which you might not be very familiar with. I know you've got free cheques in your bank account, but fork over the little extra and be grateful that this little service is available.

You're going to need a good place to hide this book. Somewhere neither your spouse nor the most curious of children will find. You will also need a quiet place to read without interruption. This book does not lend itself to being pulled out of your desk drawer at lunchtime and read with one hand while you hold a dill pickle with the other.

We are going to be talking seriously from now on, because this is serious business.

Let's go.

Contents

DEDICATION

FOREWORD

INTRODUCTION:
You Are Not Alone **xvii**
A Short Note to Anxious or
Suspicious Wives **xxi**

PART I
Putting Affairs in Their
Proper Perspective **1**

AFFAIR!

INTRODUCTION

You Are Not Alone

I don't need to tell you that extramarital sex is pretty much universally condemned. I fully expect that the mere publication of this book will be considered by many to be morally reprehensible. No one in their right mind tries to seek public approval by telling people that they are contemplating, are in or have had a clandestine extramarital affair. Extramarital affairs can be physically dangerous, financially ruinous and emotionally disastrous.

Yet in the face of this, even according to a 1994 survey by the National Opinion Research Centre at the University of Chicago, considered to be the most conservative results ever obtained, 21.2% of men and 11.3% of women admitted to having crossed the line. Marriage and family therapists consulted in the preparation of this book believe, without exception, that the actual numbers are *far* higher. They generally concur with the results of the Kinsey Report[1] which found the following infidelity rates: 50–60% of middle- and upper-income males below the age of 60 admitted to having had an extramarital affair; the rate for women in the same group was 40–50%. Other studies provide statistics falling somewhere between these two sets of data. But no matter which numbers you accept as being the most accurate, we are talking about tens of millions of people here. And extramarital affairs have *always* been with us in significant numbers.

Such being the case, it is hard to accept that such a large part of our population are moral monsters. We all know of good friends, decent people, who suddenly separate and are soon seen in the company of someone whom we can obviously tell they did not just meet last week. Assuming that they haven't used their affair as a tool to publicly humiliate their spouse (a truly creepy act), our friends remain our friends[2].

When it comes to the rich and famous, we have a *real* double standard. We participate vicariously in the peccadilloes of movie stars via tabloid newspapers and television shows. Elizabeth Taylor's notorious affair with Richard Burton while she was married to Eddie Fisher didn't hurt her appeal at the box office or her ability to market fragrances in later life. Without extramarital sex, most novelists and truckloads of screenwriters would be out of business and there would be no soap operas at all.

But when it comes to dealing with ourselves and our struggles with our own desires and needs, the seers of the legitimate world

1 Reinish, June M., PhD, *Kinsey Institute New Report on Sex*, St Martin's Press, 1991.

2 A *Time/CNN* poll which came out in August 1998 indicated that women were more forgiving of their women friends who cheat than they were of men, based on the principle that 'they wouldn't have done it unless they were provoked'. Hmmm.

turn their backs to us. The psychology sections of bookshops are filled with titles that deal with how to save, revive, reinvigorate, maintain the romance and passion in and otherwise strengthen marriage. A very large subset of these discusses how to prevent affairs from happening or repair a marriage after their revelation. (If you want to become an armchair therapist and expert on the subject, I've included an Appendix which contains an extensive but not exhaustive list. We'll have more than a few things to say about them later.) Right alongside those books, albeit substantially fewer in number, are others on how to have a successful, prosperous, healing, liberating, ennobling and happiness-producing divorce. It is a rare book indeed that deals with an extramarital affair as anything other than a dangerous animal to be hunted down and destroyed as a threat to the institution of marriage, a failure of character or a bad way of acting out some difficulty that could be better handled by therapy or litigation (which most of these authors, incidentally, dispense for a living).

No one is going to say publicly that they make money off of the more generous and festive aspects of other people's extramarital affairs. Yet they do and we respect and patronise these most glamorous of names: Cartier, Tiffany, Chanel, Dom Perignon, etc. Contrary to the images that jewellers, perfumers and furriers like to project about being there so that you can give your spouse a special anniversary gift, most would go bankrupt if the entire population became suddenly faithful.

What's going on? Why is there such a large gap between what we say and what we do? Why are such great risks being taken? Although it would be a little precious to say that there is a unique reason for each person, it would also be in error to claim that, at bottom, it is purely psychopathology. Extramarital affairs are *not* aberrations; they are part and parcel of our evolutionary biology, the development of our civilisation and the most noble and beautiful creations of human thought.

Extramarital affairs may often fulfil real emotional needs; needs that are universal and of such strength and durability as to make millions of married people willing to put their reputations, relationships and personal fortunes at risk. When properly managed, an extramarital affair can be one of the keys that unlocks the door to personal discovery, spiritual enrichment and a happier and more fulfilling life. Handled improperly, it can be the destructive, ugly disaster for which it is far better known. The path *you* follow is up to you.

A Short Note to Anxious or
Suspicious Wives

The vast majority of self-help books, with the exception of those related to careers, computers, investing or improving your golf swing, are purchased by women. So, although I expect that a fair proportion of those expecting to use this book for its intended purpose may be women, I would not be surprised if a large percentage of those reading this book (and maybe even purchasing it) fall into your category. The title alone may fill you with trepidation. As discussed elsewhere in this book, men and women often approach affairs very differently: for men, the affair is often *predominantly* about the physical aspects of sex; for women, it is *primarily* the emotional intimacy that provides the satisfaction and exhilaration that come from an affair. The betrayal that you probably fear most is an emotional one; you would probably more easily forgive an anonymous, drunken hour with a prostitute than you would a dozen intimate dinners with an attractive, articulate woman with whom your husband only held hands and nuzzled.

But let's start off with two very basic questions: a. *Why do you want to know?* and b. *What difference will it make to you if you do know?* I realise these questions sound amazingly stupid. I assure you that they are not.

Let's say, for a moment, that you no longer love your husband. If knowing will determine whether or not you wish to divorce your spouse, it is information you don't need; it is unnecessary to allege a particular violation of the marital vows in order to have standing to obtain a divorce. You may have already decided to divorce your spouse and believe that 'getting the goods' on him may get you a fatter settlement? Be careful. To the extent that you humiliate him publicly, it may negatively impact his ability to continue to earn a living at the same level or advance his career and thereby deprive you of the opportunity to collect a bigger property settlement now or greater maintenance payments in the future. Do you want to know because you are jealous of him and want to tell your children, family, friends, etc. who seem to have an inordinate amount of love and respect for him that he doesn't deserve it? Who do you think will be harmed more by this mean-spirited act?

OK. That exercise is over. You love your husband dearly; you are afraid that, even though he loves you, his passion for you has faded and that he is on the verge of looking for another woman to satisfy his desires. Do you crave reassurance of his fidelity? It can never be satisfied because, although he may be faithful today, tomorrow will have its own dynamic. And you will have established a pattern of secretly investigating your spouse – behaviour that is not conducive to generating emotional intimacy on the part of either partner. If your fear is confirmed, notwithstanding your belief that it is 'better to know,' it will only make you more miserable than you feel right now.

'Most hurt partners ... have a knack of going after information that will make them suffer. 'Do you still think about her?' 'Did you enjoy sex with her more than me?...' – these are the sorts of self-destructive questions that only drive the knife in deeper. What's the point?' [3]

The other side of the coin of uncertain fear is hope. The other side of the coin of hard knowledge is dread. If you did learn about an affair, how do you think you would react? Would it crush your spirit irremediably? Would you be so obsessed with the affair and your husband's lover that you would be unable to focus on what went wrong in your relationship and the steps you would need to take to fix it?[4] Be honest. If you feel yourself nodding 'yes', do your best to just let go.

There's another, equally important factor to consider. You don't know the status of the affair. It might well be winding down or falling apart for reasons completely unrelated to you. If you confront your spouse, he may feel cornered and defensive. Suddenly, he is put into the position of having to choose between you and his lover and your intrusive behaviour will not make you seem a more attractive choice. You may well snatch defeat from the jaws of victory.

3 Spring, Janice Abrahms, PH.D., *After the Affair*, HarperCollins, 1996, p. 179.

4 Ibid., p.250.

The controversial proposal for gays in the military, regardless of what you think of it, provides the best advice for those wondering about a straying partner: 1. Don't investigate; 2. Don't ask; and 3. (for the possibly straying spouse) Don't tell. This advice notwithstanding, you may still want to look at what will happen to you, your husband and your marriage when you confront your spouse with your concerns, suspicions or accusations. All right, then. We discuss the whole issue of disclosure in Chapter 24, Dealing With Discovery. Still, I would hope that you can see this issue for what it is: a futile exercise that will only help you make yourself feel more miserable than you already do.

It is true that *some* men crave and are fascinated by variety and there isn't much that you can do about that. This does not mean, however, that you are condemned to sit idly, worrying and waiting with the extramarital Sword of Damocles hanging over your head. Most men, though filled with sexual longings, are not born womanisers. Unlike the vast majority of women who have affairs and are emotionally torn, a significant percentage of men who have affairs are really satisfied with and *don't* want to leave their wives (as their angst-ridden, unmarried girlfriends will attest). Let's assume that your marriage is, as far as you can tell, generally *not* a basket case: you and he work as a team; your home doesn't seethe with hostility; you have a few laughs or share a conspiratorial smile in public now and then. With only a little self-discipline, you can greatly reduce the odds of an affair's destructive force. You only need the will to do it.

What will help? Ever since the White House sex scandal was reported *ad nauseam* in the US, and finally discarded as old news, this has all become somewhat easier to talk about: a commitment to becoming an adept and enthusiastic practitioner of oral sex and to gaining or regaining tone and control over your P-C muscles is a great way to start. There are lots of books and almost every issue of *Marie Claire* or *Cosmo* to tell you how to perform these two tasks admirably. If it's that simple, why is it so difficult? The problem is that, like weight loss, most people are more comfortable ruminating and making only half-hearted attempts than in really taking action. You may feel that, since it's not your 'fault' that your husband may be tempted to find sexual gratification elsewhere, it's not your obligation to make it right. If you just want to feel justified for fretting that your groom is or may become a lying weasel, that is up to you. If you really want to try to reduce the odds of an affair, undertake action cheerfully and without martyrdom. Remember, you are working for *your* health, happiness and peace of mind and not just what you think is best for him. You will feel better about your husband, your relationship *and* yourself. Good luck to you.

PART I

PUTTING AFFAIRS IN THEIR PROPER PERSPECTIVE

CHAPTER 1

Why Are Extramarital Affairs So Common and What Are They *Really*?

50–70% percent of married men and 30–50% percent of married women will have an affair sooner or later. The result is that, in 80% of all marriages, one partner or the other will be unfaithful.[5]

Almost every book I've come across that discusses affairs gets down immediately to Darwin. I've seen some that give excruciating detail on the 'adulterous' behaviour of chimpanzees, penguins and bluebirds, for goodness sake! I think a lot of them use it for 'filler.' Here's the Cliff's Notes summary, by way of the October, 1998 edition of the journal *Science*: For both males and females of virtually every species, even those

5 More estimates. These particular statistics come from *Adultery, the Forgivable Sin* by Bonnie Eaker Weil, PH.D. It would be foolish to clutter the main or footnote text with lots of unnecessary references in an effort to infuse this work with an aura of scholarship (I *know* you don't care), but I've included some notes in the Appendix which contain information that will, hopefully be found interesting or useful.

historically thought to 'mate for life' like some bird species, infidelity is a successful survival strategy and has basically been 'programmed' into our genetic makeup. Although *social* monogamy is common, *genetic* monogamy is virtually non-existent. In each species, males seek to expand their genetic influence and females seek to obtain the greatest benefits for themselves and the genetic makeup, care and survival of their offspring. Even among those bird species considered among the most monogamous of creatures, only females '... socially bonded with very high quality males'... appear to be truly faithful. And, as described in the end notes, primates rate particularly low in this department; we humans are actually the best of the primate lot. Nevertheless, our adulterous behaviour occurs with great frequency, even in our most civilised societies, despite the tremendous risks – physical, emotional and financial – to its participants.

We are, however, far more than the sum of our evolutionary biology. Chapter 4, Knowing Yourself, is devoted to examining and gaining insight into the constellation of emotional needs that drive our complex and uniquely human behaviour. It is how we demonstrate our differences as well as similarities to other species, when it comes to matters of fidelity. And, incidentally, how you will determine if and how an affair might help you become a happier and more fulfilled person.

This brings us to another obvious, but touchy subject which we will be discussing in greater detail in the next chapter. While we may be the only species capable of *morality*, it does not come naturally. Indeed, it is the very struggle between our true natures and our aspirations that is the source of great literature, art and drama (and, one must add, awful literature, art and drama). The twin titans of literature: Flaubert's *Madame Bovary* and Tolstoy's *Anna Karenina*. Prefer to read late-20th-century Americans? John Updike's *Couples* stands out. At the other end of the quality spectrum, popular though it was: *The Bridges of Madison County* and, of course, countless potboilers.

But let's answer the next question that was posed at the beginning of this section: What are extramarital affairs, *really*. Let's start with the obvious. I would hope that, by now, people would have stopped quibbling about where the line is when it comes to what constitutes an extramarital affair, but the question 'what is extramarital sex?' is not as *truly* stupid a question as it sounds. Lawyers have caused the deaths of many innocent trees by writing legal briefs and memoranda arguing this issue. The most infamous 'legally accurate' proclamation of innocence was, of course, by Bill Clinton with regard to Monica Lewinsky's playing 'Hail to the Chief' on the presidential kazoo. Lawyers and US presidents aren't the only ones to make ludicrous arguments, however: not too long ago, I recall hearing a dentist claim that he wasn't really having an affair because he used a condom and therefore he and his girlfriend weren't *actually touching*. Yeah, right.

Anyway, for our purposes, there is at least some requisite sexual contact component, be it straight, oral, anal or manual. I realise that there will be disagreements here, but let's keep it fairly close to consensus. We will deal with the issue of cyber affairs separately later on. The rest of this book will not contain a great deal of explicit discussion of sexual activity, since it presumes that any lack of adeptness on your part is not your main concern. If it is, there are lots of books, videos, etc. out there to help.

Affairs are usually of two basic types, broadly characterised as the love affair and the sex affair. The classic love affair has, at its core, an emotionally and sexually intimate bond between a married person and someone other than the spouse. It is often the stuff of great literature. A sex affair, by contrast, is a liaison between a married person and a non-spouse that involves genital contact, but little or no emotional involvement. It is often the stuff of great X-rated videos. However, even sex affairs involve some level of relationship; paid sex with a prostitute or gigolo and drunken couplings at the office Christmas bash that embarrass both participants are beneath our consideration.

Both love affairs and sex affairs have many variations (human beings are, after all, a wondrous and complex species) and we will be discussing many of these in considerable detail in Chapter 3: What's So Great About an Extramarital Affair?

Thanks to modern technology, there has recently arisen a third kind of affair, which is now becoming quite common: the Cyber Affair. In an era where intercourse has become a potentially fatal activity, the cyber affair gives new meaning to the phrase 'safe sex'. A married person will meet someone in a 'chat room' on the Internet. Internet addresses are exchanged and instant messages sent back and forth. The content usually consists of discussions of ever more intimate topics followed ultimately by explicit descriptions of sexual activity. Although it can be emotionally and (when accompanied by self-stimulation) physically gratifying, the lack of real world contact between the parties places the cyber affair beyond the scope of this book.

This book, by the way, is not for the purpose of encouraging extramarital sex. If there is one obvious truth, it is that sex needs no encouragement. As the previously cited statistics amply demonstrate, extramarital sex is doing quite nicely on its own, thank you. But, if anything is worth doing (and millions of men and women passionately believe that their affairs are, indeed, in that category), it is worth doing *well*. Well, in the broadest sense: from knowing why you want to begin an affair, what you will need to do to prepare yourself to increase the success and enjoyment of your affair, and how to use the affair to enhance rather than detract from the other aspects of your life and the lives of those closest to you, how to bring it to a satisfying conclusion, if necessary, and how to integrate it into your own spiritual growth. Nothing worthwhile comes without effort, but that effort has to be directed. The problem with most people's affairs is that they flail away wildly at them. Not the regimen of champions. But, before we get started in earnest, let's hit some of the most basic issues.

CHAPTER 2

What's So Bad About an Extramarital Affair and Why Is the Emotional Impact of an Extramarital Affair on a Marriage So Powerful?

Although this book makes absolutely no pretence at being a scholarly text, it makes obvious sense for us to discuss some of the underlying reasons why affairs receive such universal condemnation despite our widespread participation in the activity and our genetic predisposition to fool around. Absent the religious and moral strictures, being monogamous, as one psychologist noted, is a bit like losing weight; we know we should do it, but most of us lack the willpower.

It's *really* tempting to get into a discourse here on the nature of morality, but that is beyond both the scope of this book and my area of expertise. William Bennett seems to be the pop author holding forth on the subject currently and I will leave it him and others, including a pantheon of great moral philosophers, for you to read, if that is your area of interest.

Virtually every society, both primitive and advanced, has rules against having sex with a person other than the one with whom a marriage ritual has been performed. Although the rules would seem to serve both parties in a marriage, they are enforced primarily against women, probably for the reasons that are the artifacts of our discussion of evolution in the previous chapter and because men have the strength to make the rules. In many cultures, even where there is polygamy, such as in parts of Africa and the Muslim world, the men harbour such a fear of their women's unbridled sexuality that they perform genital mutilation routinely, under the euphemism of 'female circumcision'. Even so, they *still* don't trust in their faithfulness.

For most of us, the Bible has been our moral touchstone. The problem with that is that we (and just about everyone else) *use it only selectively to serve those purposes we already want to further.* Face it: if we were *really* going to follow the Bible, just by starting with the first five books of the Old Testament, everyone would have to say *adios* to baby back ribs, tattoos and visits to expensive seafood restaurants. Not likely. And we haven't even *begun* to consider Proverbs or Paul's Letters, which provide really detailed guidance for a virtuous life.

But one of the first things you will hear people say is that adultery violates the Ten Commandments and that *they* are special. Let's take a look. The Ten Commandments are divided into two sections: the duties one owes to God and the duties that one owes to fellow humans. None is mentioned as being any more important than any other. If we were to really be serious about it, going to the church or synagogue every Sabbath would be more important to us than celebrating Easter or Yom Kippur, because it is the only religious observance specifically commanded by God. But what of the duties we owe each other? Our society has reached a consensus on each of these Commandments that runs the entire spectrum beginning by *blocking* Commandments via protecting freedom of speech. What about 'Thou shalt honour thy father and thy mother'? How many autobiographies have you read where the author dumps on his or her parents? We have had a slew of popular magazines and television shows such as *Hello!* and *Lifestyles of the Rich and Famous* that fly in the face of the tenth commandment ('Thou shall not covet...'). By contrast, our society provides imprisonment or death itself for the violation of other commandments ('Thou shall not steal' and 'Thou shalt not kill'). Adultery seems to fit into that grey-area of activity just below bearing false witness and above covetousness. (By the way, the wickedness of Sodom and Gomorrah in Genesis related to tales of violent, homosexual rape, not *consensual* sexual activity as is often intoned on Sundays. When it comes to thy neighbour's spouse, Proverbs 5–7 is where the action is.) But my whole point here is that a simple reliance on abstract moral teachings is never an adequate answer for the vast majority of thinking people when considering their own circumstances.

So, what's the big deal then about what people do with their genitals in their spare time? Although Erica Jong wrote about her quest for uncomplicated sex – 'the zipless fuck' – in her book, *Fear of Flying*, in reality, it's not that simple.

The word you hear a lot is *betrayal*. It carries a certain heft with it. It is to marriage (a governmentally sanctioned institution) what treason is to the state and, considering the severity with which affairs are condemned, on the surface, at least, it's amazing that our society hasn't been completely torn asunder by the act of infidelity. And, although the way that adulterers are most commonly depicted in the media makes them seem both selfish and oblivious to the personal risks and societal condemnation, in reality, the vast majority of affairs are not entered into lightly.

'Love affairs are deadly serious, and the popular references to "playing around" are merely intended to belittle them by distortion. Perhaps life would be simpler if sex were not serious business ...but that is not how we were made. The most powerful passions in life cannot be made trivial.[6]

In truth, we may talk about adultery in the context of religious proscription to give gravity to our feelings, but what really only matters to us *are* our feelings. What causes the emotional devastation? Think gut reaction: we know that something far greater than property rights is at stake here; it is something that goes to the core of our beings, to our self-esteem and self-image. It is the stuff of our religions, myths and literature: the Bible, the *Iliad*, Medea, Camelot, *Othello* and incalculable tales of love, passion, betrayal and revenge.

Although these feelings are strong for both men and women, it is probably something each experiences in a very different way. For some women, it may even be a reaction akin to protecting the child or one's self from some grave physical danger – one must be alert to the attacks of predators if one is to survive. For the betrayed woman, even though she herself is probably a working spouse, the other woman may be seen as an immediate threat to her security and the security and patrimony of her

6 Taylor, Richard, *Love Affairs*, Prometheus Books, 1997, p. 69

children in whom she has invested years of time and may indeed have made her life's work. (It's no coincidence that a common euphemism for the threatening female is 'homewrecker'.)

This cliché remains as a carryover from an earlier age when women had far fewer life options. However, as the research cited earlier concluded, modern married women are not intrinsically more faithful than men; they will engage in extramarital affairs just as readily, if they have the freedom and the opportunity.

These evolutionary artifacts are worked out in the context of competitive sexual jealousy and in our self-esteem, the images that we have of ourselves within the social hierarchy. That competition begins way before marriage: we men often seek to quantify our sexual prowess, e.g. penis size, number of women bedded down, number of minutes between intromission and orgasm, number of orgasms within a particular amount of time, etc., to place ourselves among other men. Locker-room banter often reflects these anxieties which men commonly deal with through joking and taunting of each other. Women, on the other hand, tend to wonder qualitatively: whether the other women her man has slept with were prettier, more shapely or more sexually adventurous. They share their anxieties more readily with their friends than do men and are more upfront about their needs to seek reassurance.

Once we are married or in a 'committed relationship', however, a new set of rules takes over because we now have a particular status as sexual beings; we feel that we have acquired an undivided interest in each other's sexual functions as surely as we own our home as joint tenants with right of survivorship. And, as everyone knows, you can't sell your interest in your house without your spouse's consent! But, we also know that our 'ownership' of our spouse's sexuality is limited: a man may not rape his wife and, the knife-wielding Lorena Bobbitt notwithstanding, a woman may not mutilate her husband; and neither spouse can stop the other from masturbating. Obviously, it's not *just* sexual activity; it's *emotional* commitment. But where do we draw the line? Numerous emotional ties are shared with relatives, friends, confidants. The sexual element is what makes it different. And here, men and women often part company in their opinions: as mentioned in the Note to Wives, women tend to have a greater fear about their spouses' emotional intimacy with another; men's anxieties more often dwell on their wives' physical favours being shared.

Yet adultery is hardly the only marital betrayal. Our sexual lives are only part of the web of interrelating trusts that makes up a marriage. There are so many times in a marriage where major steps are taken without mutual agreement or consent and some of these common betrayals can be far more destructive than an undiscovered, clandestine affair; such as when one spouse:

- 'accidentally' foists an unwanted child upon the other through sabotaged contraception
- unilaterally invites a friend or relative to live in the household for an indefinite duration
- makes a large, surprise purchase or investment that brings financial hardship to the family

What really are the worst things about an extramarital affair? Spouses who are affair participants talk about the guilt (because the affair was entered into without the critical introspection beforehand that is absolutely vital, if one is to handle it successfully), the loss of intimacy or some other impact on the marriage. They say these things, often in retrospect, because the truth is an uncomfortable one. The second worst thing for those involved in an affair is the stress that lovers experience in trying to maintain their affair's secrecy (naturally, a significant portion of this book is devoted to helping you successfully manage this issue both internally and externally) and the *worst* thing about an affair is BEING FOUND OUT. Indeed, it is an affair's revelation, *not* its occurrence, that usually does the damage: the obsessive rage and self-pity of the spouse who feels betrayed precipitate the acts that are the primary destroyers of a marriage.[7]

Obviously, one of the most important issues that you will be struggling with is the ethics of infidelity. Every thoughtful person who becomes involved with someone outside of their marriage (and the vast majority of those who do are, indeed, thoughtful) usually examines the moral nuances of his or her particular situation very carefully. Such self-examination is critical if the affair is to stand any chance at all of being a positive experience. In Part II of this book, you will be provided with some tools to examine the ethical issues of several common marital situations and advice on how to prevent or deal successfully with the potential downsides of an affair. But first let's look at an affair's upsides (not as obvious as you would imagine).

7 Interestingly, two-thirds of 'betrayed' spouses decide to stay married. Why? Probably because, once their wounded pride was under control, those betrayed knew that they would be worse off divorced. Indeed, they are right: 80% of those who did choose to leave regretted it. These sobering statistics were the underpinnings for our recommendation in the Note to Wives to *leave their fears alone.*

CHAPTER 3

What's So Great About an
Extramarital Affair?

As we alluded to earlier, in every society, people take big, big risks to consummate a passionate attraction. There must be a reason. After all, we don't often leap into irrationality: we shake our heads in sorry disbelief at the fools who take out a second mortgage on the house to gamble in the hope of winning the big lottery jackpot, for example. We balance our needs and desires against the depths of our fears and their likelihood of realisation. The logical conclusion: affairs may be looked down upon by society and carry with them some potentially great personal costs, but, judging from our behaviour, they are *really* gratifying.

Let's start out by talking about sex affairs, if only because they usually have fewer and less complex components.

1. The Obvious (for men, at least): Quantity and Variety

A story is told about the dour US President Calvin Coolidge and his wife who, while travelling around the country, stopped at a poultry farm. Mrs Coolidge noted the copulating energy of the rooster and asked the farmer how many times a day he performed. 'Forty or fifty times a day, ma'am,' the farmer replied.

'Tell that to the President,' she said.

When the farmer had done so, President Coolidge asked,'Does the rooster always mate with the same hen?'

'Never, sir, always with a different one,' the farmer replied.

'Tell that to Mrs Coolidge,' he responded.

Variety is a pretty powerful male stimulant. There is no sexual excitement that quite matches the thrill of youthful passion that can be regained in an extramarital affair. The male brain is a strange thing when it comes to sex. I've had many friends in their forties tell me that a really sexy time with their wives enabled them to do it two or three times in one day. When these same men started an affair, however, six or seven orgasms in a 24-hour period seemed to be pretty common. Call it the 'Coolidge effect'.

In addition, for both men and women, the sex in a sex affair is qualitatively different from marital sex because it is stripped away from the activities and locale of everyday life that otherwise surround it when you make love with your spouse. In its pure and isolated form, it seems far more passionate, in part because your focus is only on pleasing and being pleased by your lover.

2. A Special Treat

Our lives often go through positive transitions, such as a promotion or the receipt of an award. With success comes a new sense of competence. And, with this upbeat feeling, we get a desire to be with someone who is appreciative, easy to please and *fun*. As sex affairs, these are usually casual, ego-enhancing experiences, lasting less than a year, and, since they are rarely discovered, seldom disrupt a marriage.

3. Sexual Adventure: The Heroic Romance of a Clandestine Affair

Most of us live fairly mundane lives. We aren't secret agents, astronauts, S.W.A.T.-team members, sports heroes, supermodels or movie stars. We know of these glamorous, exciting people and live their lives vicariously through the media. We crave heroic, glamorous romance for ourselves. Affairs by their very nature are dangerous and risky, and, if we get involved in a dangerous liaison, we become, in our own little world, heroes and heroines of a real-life adventure. This is exhilarating in a way that an amusement-park ride (which, hopefully, only gives the *illusion* of danger) can never be, because it engages the full spectrum of our emotions, abilities, personalities and wishes.

Let's admit that there are also other, less healthy, types of sex affairs, and these are the ones most often paraded out by the media: 'one night stand'-type sexual conquests where the affairee's name is not known or remembered. These acts are committed by people who are not happy: they are trying to prove something to themselves, or in an effort to banish self-doubt or express anger. The affair provides self-esteem and a sense of power that is mixed in with the self-doubt, pride, relief, regret, hostility, loneliness or whatever other emotion is really driving them.

Love affairs are quite different from sex affairs in that the sexual intimacy is accompanied by emotional intensity. But love affairs are not necessarily completely separate from sex affairs in their development. What may start out as just a 'good-time sex affair' can evolve into a powerful bond, if the participants find emotional resonance with their affair partners. What can love affairs offer that sex affairs usually do not?

1. Bridge Over Troubled Water.
This is the 'other side of the coin' of the special treat sex affair. Sometimes we just need help – support, comfort and reassurance – through some troubling time, a family tragedy, a job loss or other disappointment. Such affairs, unless they blossom, are short-lived, usually lasting less than a year and, because they, too, are rarely discovered, seldom disrupt a marriage.

2. An Alternative Life
We make choices every day. With each choice we make, others are foreclosed. For every door we open in front of us, we lock one behind us. We look at our domestic situation and wonder, sometimes wistfully, sometimes bitterly 'what if ...' or 'if only ...' An affair provides a controlled situation in which we can examine alternative lives and evaluate choices that we might have made. We can try on or experiment with

different aspects of our personalities with someone who does not know us in the context of our everyday lives. We can learn about ourselves – our needs, our potential to change or previously unknown abilities which might enable us to accomplish new things we might never have thought possible.

3. A Sensual Relationship

While primarily sexual, a sensual love affair has a sensitivity and caring aspect about it. The lovers do care about and like each other, even if not much time is spent in conversation. They experiment with everything from massage oils to whipped cream and are delighted when they find a new position or play a new game. Usually, such affairs are seen as unrelated to their 'real', married relationship. These affairs provide excitement, fantasy, thrill, pleasure, delight and eroticism, like sex affairs, but they also provide self-esteem and a sense of acceptance. Sensual affairs are often of long duration because they are seen by the lovers as being psychically beneficial and because the lovers make no demands upon each other's time or emotions.

4. Comfort for the Soul – the Loving Affair

The *Chicken Soup for the Soul* money factory has not yet published an uplifting collection of stories directed to extramarital lovers. Perhaps because lovers don't need to hear other people's touching *vignettes de liaisons*. Navigating our way through life is a difficult passage, but partners in a loving affair often make the best of it, because they know that love is, by far, the most satisfying component of living. If a successful marriage is one that involves the mutual fulfillment of needs, a loving affair can provide that extra nourishment that a poor marital choice has not. The loving affair can be an affair at its best: one based on friendship, caring and understanding and providing a refuge from the duties, pressures and responsibilities of everyday life. That sustenance can enable us to carry on with dignity and grace when the weight of our burdens seems almost more than we can bear. A loving affair, like the alternative life, also offers opportunities for self-discovery, sexual experimentation and appreciation. Even though, in many instances, the affair partners don't seriously consider leaving their spouses, loving affairs may last years, decades or even a lifetime!

5. The In-Love Affair

These are the affairs of grand passion, euphoria and pain; they are intense, compelling and compete directly with the marriage for the lives of the participants. They carry the highest risk and often lead to either a union 'with the person I've been waiting for all of my life', or an agonising break-up of the relationship. It's the high-wire act of love.

6. The Love–Hate Affair

Just as with sex affairs, love affairs can be of a truly unhealthy type: some men or women will enter into sexual affairs because they really hate the opposite sex and want to use the affair to deliver pain, humiliation and disappointment. They start by pumping up their affairee, then they gradually disappoint, frustrate, subjugate and manipulate their partner. They take money, time, energy and self-esteem from their lover. What's in it for them? They derive a sense of safety through domination and control. *This* book is not for them. And, as we discuss in Chapter 9, Finding, Evaluating and Choosing Your Lover, *they* are not for you.

Each of us has his or her own unique background, circumstances, needs and desires that a good affair may help satisfy. It is up to you, with the help of this book, to understand your own needs and determine what kind of an affair is right for you, if, indeed, it is to be seriously pursued.

PART II

YOUR EXTRAMARITAL AFFAIR

SECTION A

Making the Decision to Have an
Extramarital Affair

THIS IS A *DECISION!?!* When it comes to matters such as these, powerful, unconscious forces can often play such a strong role that intellectual, analytic activity seems to take a hike into a deep forest with scant chance of returning before dawn.

Many times, an affair is not at all planned or planned out: the onset is sudden – the old 'love-at-first-sight' or 'struck by the thunderbolt'.

Joy B., 32, married twelve years, two children: *I could've bet anyone a million dollars that I would never ever cheat on my husband. I love my husband a lot, but I don't consider him to be my soul mate – I never believed that 'soul mate' stuff. Then, one day, I met my soul mate. He made me feel like I was the most beautiful woman on earth. I've never experienced so much passion in my life. We had so much in common; we laughed, joked, talked. He was a dream come true.*

Rick D., 36, married 10 years and father to two children, *laid his whole dilemma right out on the table:*
 My wife and I are both in our mid-thirties and are healthy and relatively attractive. She stopped working a few years ago to care for the kids and our relationship has been pretty strong. We make love at least once a week and I think it is fulfilling for us both. I have a side job as a musician playing every weekend at different bars. Very recently, I met someone who, at first sight, left me literally speechless. Every guy fantasises about the attributes of his 'perfect girl'. I was staring at her and I couldn't talk. I eventually gained composure and chatted a bit with her ... nothing but small talk. She started coming every week to our gigs and we started flirting — but it was very public, very light-hearted flirting that was meant more in fun than in reality. I had done this with many friends and co-workers all my life and have seen others exhibit the same behaviour. I thought nothing of it, but I did fantasise about her. Last month, my wife went away for the weekend with the kids. At our gig that weekend, I had a few drinks, which I normally don't do, and teased the crowed that I was a bachelor this weekend. Later that evening on one of our breaks, she came up and asked me to take her home. I didn't answer right away, but, eventually, I agreed. I took her home and we spent the night together. The entire time, my mind and my pulse were racing but, at first, my body wouldn't 'co-

operate'. I told her flat out that I was still in love with my wife and this was my conscience at work. We still managed to have sex several times that night. Nevertheless, she said it was one of the best and most fulfilling nights she ever had. She is truly into doing many more different things sexually than my wife is, but we didn't have time to do 'all' that she talked about. She says she is not interested in ruining my marriage but is content to be my part-time mistress and would be extremely discreet. She would like to get together occasionally to have sex. I find myself thinking about getting together with her for the same reasons. She is on my mind a lot. So what do I do? I'm officially in 'lust' with this beautiful girl and part of me wants to explore the possibilities. I'm feeling pangs of excitement that I haven't felt since I was a teenager. On the other hand, I have every intention of living out my life with my wife, who I still love a lot. She does her best to take care of all of my needs, sexually, emotionally and spiritually. I know deep down that it's not fair to her.

For others, what starts out as an acquaintance becomes a friendship and then grows, with a natural urgency, into passion. This is especially likely when the seeds have been planted and only await the right conditions:

Sammi T., 29, married four years, no children: *It wasn't supposed to have happened this way. I have been seriously attracted to this man now for over two years and, until recently, we had done nothing about it except flirt. Two months ago, we decided it was time to get together and now I am deeply in love with him. There is not one minute in a day that I am not thinking about him. The day I married my husband, I knew it was the wrong thing to do. I have never loved him the way a wife should love her husband. I was deeply hurt from two previous relationships (one of them I had been married to) and I promised myself NEVER to love again, that way there would be no chance of getting hurt. My husband is a good person and does everything in his power to please me, but the fact is I just don't love him.*

Like many of us, Joy and Rick struggle with their feelings, trying to understand them. However, although contrary to the romantic notion of women being 'swept off their feet', Sammi's situation is what happens most typically. Half of the women in a 1992 US study by Dr Lynn Atwater knew their affair partners for several months before beginning their affair; most of the rest knew their partner a year or more. A quarter of the women surveyed said that they initiated the affair, and half said the decision was 'mutual'. On average, most of those women considered having an affair at least a month before it began and, quite often, discussed it with a friend. In this respect, women are often more thoughtful about affairs than men, some of whom, to put it more politely than they probably deserve, are content to live with the mystery of Eros.

John D., 45, married eighteen years, two children: *I have had many affairs and have wondered why I do the things I do. I have come to the conclusion that, right or wrong, that is my way; a character flaw, if you will. My wife and I both think that there is nothing wrong with our relationship; we are comfortable financially, we have a marvellous sex life and there is no reason, other than weakness, why I should sleep with other women. She knew of some of my infidelities in the past and, although they have caused problems, we have worked through them. However, I know within myself that, if I met a lady who attracted me and the opportunity arose, I would be unfaithful again. Regardless of that, I would never stop loving my wife and look forward to spending the rest of my life with her. It's a quirk of nature that sometimes lust is stronger than love or just a weakness that I can't control. It's not something that I am proud of, but also not something I am ashamed of. It's me.*

If you've already been swept away by an unexpected passion or are in the midst of a well-considered relationship, the steps you should follow and the decisions which you face (and they are many) are dealt with in later chapters. For the time being, we'll talk to those who are, just speaking metaphorically of course, strapped into their hang-gliders and curiously peering over the edge of the Grand Canyon.

CHAPTER 4

Knowing Yourself.
Why did you buy this book?

D o you just want to nail your Britney Spears-yummy baby-sitter and get away with it? Do you fantasise the steps you'll have to take to have a torrid weekend tryst with that hunk in the shipping department while your hubby is away on a fishing trip with his mates? Yuck. You are, I hope, a small minority.

No, I am speaking to the rest of you: those who have both conscience and courage. You will need both of them to face some of the big issues that you *should* face before you can determine (1) if your situation is one which may justify the risks of an affair and (2) whether you are the kind of person who will also be able to appreciate its rewards. First, you have to acknowledge to yourself that you do, indeed, have those issues. You have to understand why you are seriously contemplating charting this dangerous course today, when, some time ago, you had walked down the aisle to spend the rest of your life with the person of your heart's desire.

Your first major issue then is what, indeed, *is* your heart's desire? What are your needs? What do you value? What do you plan to do with the life that most of us think is our only time on this planet?

We all learned in school that the necessities for life are food, clothing and shelter. To have a life that is fulfilling and meaningful, however, two more ingredients are necessary: love and work. Love and work in the broadest sense. Playboys and partygirls are called 'boys' and 'girls' and not 'men' and 'women' for a reason; their ostensibly pleasurable lives do not contain the ingredients that give them meaning and they do not remain happy for very long. At the same time, few of us are called to a fulfilling, meaningful life in the way that Gandhi, Churchill or Mother Teresa were called. Our needs, wishes and values, while more modest, are more universally shared and often just as strong. You will need to take a look at them and yourself before you begin to even plan your voyage.

1. The need for physical intimacy

How important *is* physical intimacy? Consider this: a recently completed study covering a large sample of men and women followed over a 30-year period showed that hugging, kissing and other forms of physical intimacy given to a child from the very beginning of its life was by far the strongest indicator of happiness and success later on. It even enabled those fortunates to overcome many of the ill effects related to their parents' divorces, the loss of a loved one and life's disappointments in general.

This need for a loving touch does not go away with the end of childhood; it stays with us. For adults, a caring sexuality is a key ingredient to a contented and joyful life. When many of us think of an extramarital affair, it is often in those terms.

Felicia, 32, married six years, no children: *My husband and I don't have the most active sex life in the world; in fact, it's null and void these days. He's just not the 'touchy-feely' type, I guess, and he comes from a family who is the same way. Sex is at the very bottom of the list when he describes a marriage. Unfortunately, I have an extremely high sex drive for a female. (Isn't it usually the opposite? Female refuses, male always wants 'it'?) I have considered cheating, but have never set out to do so. It is hard though when a great-looking guy pays loads of attention to you when you're not getting it at home. Suffice it to say, some days it wouldn't hardly take a 'brush' by a particularly attractive man to make me forget my vows! Some people say to talk to your spouse about it, but I've done that, and he didn't listen for long. I love my husband very much, and he provides all my needs (except sexual ones). He's very handsome, has a great body, and we make a beautiful couple, I must admit. But, and I'm ashamed a bit to say this, I might consider an affair, if I had the opportunity.*

Patty D., married ten years, two children, finally acted on her frustration: *My marriage is, well, blah. I've tried everything short of asking my husband if he's gay to get him to make love to me. So, unfortunately, when a very attractive (and older) man, who is in a stale 19-year-old marriage, came along, we took quite an interest in each other. We both love our spouses and would die for each one of them. We just get NO AFFECTION at home from them. We have become very close, good friends, and the sex with him is, frankly put, WOW!! We definitely put smiles on each other's face. But we couldn't bear to leave our families. It's tough to have to get what you need outside the home. Some people might think that women like me just don't try with our husbands, but that's not true at all. Like I said, I've tried everything. I'm pretty darned good looking and sometimes I feel like I'm going to waste, being for all intents and purposes, alone in my bed at night, even though my husband is beside me.*

In our Darwinian culture of survival-of-the-fittest, we are brought up on the mantra of self-reliance. This spills over into our marriages, the one place where we seek refuge from the world. Even though we may share our lives with someone every day, some of us are still reluctant to voice our needs or are embarrassed to hear the needs of others. A large number of us are too shy or ashamed to say to our spouse how much we might long to share with them gentle caresses and passionate kisses of the most intimate places of our bodies. Some of us have even internalised the lesson of self-reliance to the point where we shut down our own awareness of our desires. It is a happy couple indeed that has two partners who are emotionally aware and are both comfortable enough to voice their wishes as the spirit moves them.

Maureen, 43, married fifteen years, two children: *My husband and I like to do it "puppy-style" because there are so many options: me lying on a stack of pillows or standing against the bed and then lying down on it; on the stairs, me kneeling or standing; lying facing down over the ottoman; lying face down on the deck while standing in the Jacuzzi; lying face down completely flat on the bed, my legs together; standing bent slightly at the waist, hanging on to something. His caressing hands coupled with the feeling of being impaled on his hard cock can be excruciatingly exquisite!! Our motto: Be creative. Be enthusiastic. And if it feels good ... DO IT!*

However, like Felicia, many of us love our spouses dearly, but still find ourselves gazing longingly at strangers: they become the imagined lovers whose awareness of the need for intimacy and level of desire more closely matches our own. For others, the lack of physical intimacy can turn first to frustration and then to the anger and bitterness that can lead to love's demise.

Weston, 39, married twenty years, three children: *My wife and I started dating in high school and stayed with each other through our junior year in college and then got married. During the time before the wedding, sex was not an issue; it was literally any time either of us wanted and she asked as much as I did and seemed to enjoy it a lot. I thought that was great and honestly was part of why I married her. After we got married, things got slower and slower and she appeared to enjoy it less and less. She now tells me she doesn't like sex, never really liked it that much, did it as a chore to please me, and now doesn't see it as a need; she can live without it, so I should, too. There is a real thread of 'female deceit' – Do it like a rabbit in the name of romance until you catch a husband and then cut the poor bastard off!*

Since physical intimacy is at the core of an affair, as well as a marriage, you need to start by honestly assessing what your *own* sexual needs are and how open you are and have been in making those needs known to your spouse. If you haven't been able to share your feelings at home, how can you be so sure that you will be able to share them in a potential lover's arms?

2. Emotional intimacy – Esteem, support and empathy

We all need to have a mirror held up to ourselves that tells us that we are worth loving: attractive, perhaps, or smart, funny, caring, insightful, etc. We also need someone who will help us shoulder our heavier burdens without judging us for needing their help. And we need to feel that someone understands what we ourselves feel to confirm that our feelings have merit. These are needs that are rooted in childhood and stay with us in one form or another, often under heavy disguise, for the rest of our lives. Rare is the one relationship that can fulfil these needs for both parties.

If you are, indeed, contemplating an affair, do you know which needs aren't being met in your marriage? This is a good time to do an important self-assessment. Rank the needs that you feel are the most important to fulfilling you as a person. Most important first, least last. Include those which relate to work, hobbies, children, extended family, friends, etc., as well as to your spouse, not just esteem, support and empathy.

Here's a sampling of some of the kinds of needs you might feel are important (and, by the way, don't be ashamed to call them 'needs' rather than 'wants' or 'desires'. Too self-critical. The human heart needs what it wants):

• An adventurous, pleasurable and satisfying sex life
• Recognition for achievement or position in your work
• Financial wealth or security
• Love and admiration of your spouse, family and friends
• Achieving some level of excellence in a sport or hobby
• Standing in the community, 'fame'
• Spiritual peace; closeness with God; time for reflection, etc.
• Healthy body
• Physical attractiveness

Which of those needs are or could be impacted by your spouse? Are they among your highest priority needs? Which could, in theory, be met by the 'ideal spouse'? [8] Surely your spouse is particularly strong in meeting at least *some* of the needs you listed as being important! Now review the list and see which needs aren't being met. Are they the most important ones, sort of in the middle or far down the list? Let's say that the most important, unsatisfied needs are near the top of the list. Now, when you think about having a lover and all that that means, which and how many of these unmet needs, in your honest opinion, would a relationship with him or her be highly likely

8 To my gentlemen readers: let's not get silly here, guys. No asking for a Jordan lookalike who has the investment savvy of Warren Buffet and can help you have a golf swing like Tiger Woods.

to satisfy? If your answer is all or virtually all, no wonder you find yourself fantasising about an affair or reading this book in the hope that you will discover a path to greater fulfilment and happiness! Later on, in Chapter 8, we'll discuss the qualities you will have to develop (if you don't have them already) in order to successfully move in the direction you need to go. But, for now, let's discuss the most practical obstacle between you and your new love – your spouse – in our next chapter.

CHAPTER 5

Knowing Your Spouse

Men marry women hoping that they won't change.
Women marry men hoping that they will.

There are lots of blockbuster bestsellers by Ph.D.s on how men and women perceive, behave and communicate differently (John Gray of *Mars and Venus* fame had a good run as the celebrity academic *du jour* on the subject). They can explain these differences far better than I can. But the quote above by that ancient sage, Anonymous, is not about perceptions, communications or relating; it is about our powerful, but unspoken, expectations.

When a man marries a woman, he is usually thinking about *her:* what she looks, smells, feels and sounds like; and how he feels when he is with her: proud, virile, protective, admired, desired, etc.[9] He is marrying a *current, but necessarily temporary, reality.*

9 Donald Trump once commented about a supermodel he was dating (what other kind would he date): 'I go into a restaurant 'I go into a restaurant with her and grown men weep.'

She, on the other hand, is often imagining their life together: the place they will live, how they will interact on a daily basis, how they will raise children, have a social life, talk about their daily lives, i.e. a *possible future reality*. The more granular and detailed the fantasy, the less likely that it will come true exactly.

Much has been written about how the story of *Cinderella* has such a hold on girls and does not let go even after their marriage to a man who is less than a Prince Charming (and we all are) should shatter the illusion. Women who hold fast to this illusion seem to conveniently forget that to get the full-Disney Prince Charming, you have to be the full-Disney Cinderella, i.e. drop-dead gorgeous, cheerful, able to readily communicate with birds and rodents and obediently perform hard manual labour for years on end without complaint.

How are these unrealistic expectations by both parties so often played out? Since the man's romantic attachment is to the woman who no longer exists, he seeks to find that woman; since the woman's reality did not match her fantasy, she seeks the missing pieces in another man.

This doesn't usually happen within hours after vows are exchanged, of course. When it does, it's called marital fraud, as, for example, where a man has told his bride-to-be that he wants to have lots of children, but has secretly had a vasectomy. What usually happens is not that the couple's expectations get violated, which is inevitable, but that they are violated at a rate that is faster than one to which they can adjust because they have not yet created the deeper attachment that will see them through those disappointments.

No reasonable man will honestly say that he expects his wife to have a strong libido, smooth, elastic skin, flat stomach, firm breasts, etc. on the occasion of their 50th anniversary. Few brides of young men just beginning their careers would reasonably expect a 7,000 sq ft house with a Mercedes 600 SL in the circular, gated driveway, by the time that they turned 30. But a woman who doubles her weight within the first five years of marriage or a man who decides that work just isn't his 'thing', is bound to stir up within his or her spouse feelings of disappointment bordering on outrage. It may not legally be considered marital fraud, but it sure *feels* like it.

These are, obviously, extreme examples, but they illustrate our gut reactions to their milder manifestations. Your wife may claim that she tries to watch her weight, but, if there is a half-eaten large container of fudge ripple ice cream in the house, you are probably feeling strangely betrayed. If you have told your husband that you crave romance and he responds with laughter punctuated by a loud belch and asks, 'How's that?', you feel more than a little diminished. Now what?

If we are to overcome our strong drive for genetic promiscuity and allow monogamy to triumph, we and our spouses have an implicit obligation to each other to meet each other's needs to the best of our abilities. If you buy into the quote that began this chapter, it means that the wife has an obligation to try to be the woman she purported to be when her husband fell in love with her, and the man has an obligation to use his best efforts to fulfil her reasonable expectations. For both of you, this means hard work, dedication and honest communication about really touchy subjects. It is not easy and I would urge you to look at the myriad of books that seek to assist in this activity, if you haven't already done so. Go ahead. This book will still be here when you've done it.

However, you may indeed have already attempted such actions and it may well be that you sincerely believe that your unhappy circumstances will not, and cannot, change; *that* is probably the reason why you're reading this book. But an affair is not, obviously, the only answer, so let's move on to discuss that other alternative in our next chapter.

CHAPTER 6

Reviewing Your Efforts to Either Improve or End Your Marriage

Reading this book with serious intent is a major step. Why? Because, despite your best efforts, the odds that an affair will adversely impact your marriage are not insignificant. When you were thinking about your own needs and how your spouse did or did not meet them, as we discussed in the preceding chapters, was getting a divorce very much in the forefront of your mind?

After all, having an affair in order to precipitate a divorce is like driving into a tree in order to stop a car. There are a lot cheaper, less traumatic and less messy ways to accomplish the same result. And, believe me, an uncovered affair is extremely likely to precipitate a divorce. As we will be discussing later on, the odds are very high that, once discovered, you would *never* be truly forgiven by your spouse. Your affair will *always* be waiting in the wings of their thoughts, ready to be thrown at you at the slightest provocation, used against you in the midst of a disagreement or just out of the blue.

As I mentioned in the previous chapter, there are a lot of books about improving your marriage, bringing back the romance, preventing your marriage from deteriorating into a divorce, etc. (I've listed a few in the Appendix. See which ones resonate best with you.) *Marie Claire* and *Cosmo* and just about every other mass-market women's magazine in the shops have become the monthly relationship fix-it manuals for women, and *Men's Health, GQ* and *Esquire* are jumping on the bandwagon, too.

When it comes to trying to save or improve your marriage, have you communicated your feelings to your spouse? Did she or he get defensive or go ballistic? Just stare blankly? Accuse you of dastardly deeds while you are still innocent? Have you gone down the counselling route and hit a dead end?

If, after *genuine* effort, and *serious* introspection, you do not love your spouse enough and believe that there is not a precious enough relationship there to want to spend the rest of your lives together *and* that there are no compelling practical reasons to stay temporarily, you *should* leave. You owe it to your spouse as much as yourself to both have the opportunity to enjoy reciprocated love during the remainder of your and your spouse's time here on earth. Forget what family and friends will think. If they speak badly of you, it will only be for their own base motives. Dr Diane Medved, in her book *The Case Against Divorce*, gave four components which, when present for several months, mean it's time to bail out:

1. Your day-to-day relationship is so punishing or unbearable that your functioning is impaired.

2. You strive to be away from your spouse as much as possible.
3. You would rather be alone than married to your spouse.
4. Your values and your spouse's diverge irreconcilably.

And these reasons are, of course, in addition to the *real* no-brainers of drug abuse, psychosis, mental or physical abuse and just not being able to stand married life one more minute.

If you *do* decide to go forward with a divorce, jump ahead to Chapter 22, where we discuss briefly some of the basics of how to prepare financially and tactically to get the best outcome.

CHAPTER 7

Three Common Situations that Serve as an Appropriate Basis for Going Forward with an Extramarital Affair

I f you are at the point where you are seriously interested in what follows here, you have probably spent a large chunk of the recent past 'if only-ing'. Some of us look back on our hopes and expectations with a bitter laugh. We imagined eternal youth and ardour then, and only now have begun to feel the gravity of the words intoned at our weddings: '... for better or worse ...'. No one grows up daydreaming about the rosy future in which they will be *ensconced in a relationship that makes them miserable to the point of desperation.*

In previous chapters, you took the opportunity to recognise and prioritise the aspects of life that matter the most in contributing to your happiness. You also assessed where your spouse fits in to that evaluation. Despite your best efforts and those of which you believe your spouse to be capable (for the time being, at least), you have come to the inescapable conclusion that the kind of marriage that you need cannot be built from the marriage you have. That is a lot – more than enough for now.

You may lament meeting your spouse or having been foolish or careless enough to have had children with him or her. You may also berate yourself for not having left 'when you had the chance'. Forget the woulda-shoulda-couldas. Our mistakes are to be learned from, not to be used for self-abuse. The best time for thoughtful analysis of your life's major themes and patterns is when you are at peace. That time will come.

Having examined your current set of circumstances, what you must do now is (1) have the sincere desire to do the right thing for your own fulfilment and happiness and the happiness of those around you, (2) have the courage to make decisions which will lead you to fulfilment and (3) have the commitment to do your best to see your decisions through to their successful result. If your actions are driven by jealously, greed, the desire for revenge or other base motives, you will fail, and the mess you make will be of *epic* proportions. Some people actually want that. If you do, too, you're a couch candidate and I can't help you.

If our lives were stripped of their complexities, our choices would be easy: two young, physically and emotionally healthy people with no children and little money who just happened not to be *simpatico* could divorce so quickly they'd leave skidmarks on the way to court. They often do and their numbers are legion. They are also probably not reading this book (or this chapter, at least).

No, ma'am. No, sir. Our lives are sticky. We have legal and

moral responsibilities. We have values and needs that are mutually exclusive of total fulfilment. (Wouldn't we all just love to have a meaningful, fascinating job, a passionate love life, more time with our children and be able to pursue hobbies, make new friends, learn new skills, appreciate nature, music and art, and improve our spiritual and physical well-being, all at once?) We have to make choices and compromises and find the mix that adequately satisfies both our personal needs and what our conscience calls upon us to do as right. For many of us, having gone through the marriage assessment discussed earlier, the answer cannot simply be to say to our spouse, and maybe our children, 'See ya.'

There can be many situations where the balance of personal fulfilment and the moral responsibility to take care of and nurture those closest to you place the extramarital affair, rather than divorce or the insufferable status quo, at the centre of the equation. Although only you can assess what is right for your circumstances, there is usually one of three basic reasons that place unhappily married people in situations where the extramarital affair arguably makes the most sense.

1. The Emotional Well-being of Your Children

A two-parent family, living in *adequate* harmony, is the greatest gift you can give your kids. Forget Drs. Albert Schweitzer and Martin Luther King, Jr. The melding of love and work that gives meaning to life for most of us is our children. Our daily sacrifices are silent (and sometimes not-so-silent) testament to it. Long after the applause we receive for landing the big account, winning an academic prize, gaining a sought-after position or writing a book has faded away, the memory of the embrace of one's own child remains.

Our evolutionary biology as well as the history of civilisation bear out the importance of growing up in households of both fathers and mothers. In the societal groupings of virtually all higher-order primates, juveniles have regular interactions with both adult males and females. It is in the nuclear family that (1) children learn about relating as men and women to men and women, (2) they learn to deal with their own feelings of identity and sexuality and (3) they get the sense of completeness that comes from being exposed to both halves of the human equation.

'The kids could see we weren't happy together. What kind of role model for marriage is that? They're better off with one parent than two miserable ones, even if that one parent is struggling.'

When people want to get divorced, they tend to rationalise the benefits to the children. Don't buy it: in order for a child to actually be better off with one parent than with two, the parent that leaves has to be a pretty terrible parent and not just one the custodial spouse doesn't care for very much any more. Furthermore, custody, visitation and childrearing questions can cause conflict far more bitter than anything that happened under the commonly shared roof. After all, now there's money for lawyers at stake and the forum of the courts in which to play out the wounds to one's ego. No one will seriously contend that the children are better insulated from pain by having gone through the divorce process. They should be spared this trauma while they are young for as long as possible.

Do you have the grit, love and generosity to stay in and make the best of a bad marriage at least until the children are older? Although it isn't always recognised, practically all of the fighting that takes place between parents is the spillover of the frustration and anger they feel when their needs – for affection, recognition, security, etc. – are not being met. Rarely is the matter of disagreement actually about peripheral issues, such as whether the children should watch one hour or three hours of TV a night or whether they should go to church every Sunday instead of playing with their friends; mostly that's a smokescreen and *you* have to cut through that haze.

If, despite the bad marriage, our children are to be tended in an adequately harmonious environment, the anger and frustration must abate. When the spouse is unable or unwilling to meet those needs and you have, notwithstanding your best efforts, been unable to ameliorate the situation within the marital context, the clandestine extramarital affair can provide the personal satisfaction necessary to enable you to be less argumentative, more giving and tolerant, and a better spouse and parent. You may take at least some comfort in the knowledge that the circumstances are temporary and that there *is* a light at the end of the tunnel. Less than your personal ideal? Of course. But the dividends that will be reaped in your children's lives will be worth it.

I can already hear people screaming; 'YOU ARE TEACHING YOUR CHILD, BY YOUR EXAMPLE, TO BE A LYING CHEAT!!' Give it a rest. If we are honest, we will realise that the volume of the scream is unrelated to our concern for the pedagogical aspects of the act. It is the identification with the 'wronged' spouse in our imagination that is doing the screaming. Anyone who has raised children with all of the honesty they can muster will attest to the fact that their children will spontaneously dissemble. If a toddler, happily absorbed in play, is asked if she has a dirty nappy, she will say 'No!', not because she is a liar, but because she has learned that, when she says 'Yes', her play is interrupted.

Honesty *is* a virtue, but only one of many worth teaching. We also know that honesty can hurt: we often see it used by adults as a weapon, and sometimes they hide behind courtliness or the pretence of caring when they employ it. My favourite is the old 'bless his/her heart', as in: 'She certainly doesn't do anything for that dress, even though it *was* expensive, bless her heart.'

It is also our job to instil empathy and kindness in our children and, as part of that, we teach them how and when to lie from a very young age: I remember taking my two-year-old to Toys R US to buy him a football. We were served by a 60-year-old-plus woman at the checkout. As I picked up the plastic bag and took the receipt, my son boomed out, 'Good-bye, Old Lady!' The woman, who had been beaming at him while I was digging around in my wallet, suddenly looked as if she had been slapped. I made a mental note that, sometime before his fourth birthday, we were going to have to teach our boy tact.

The issues that arise with your children will revolve around your relationship and how much time you spend with *them*, and *not* around your extramarital affair. (I do not recall ever hearing of a father, who, upon returning home, was asked by his child, 'Who caressed your genitals today?' and lamented having to give the false answer, 'No one but Mummy, kiddo!') If you are a loving and actively engaged parent, it is only the *revelation* of your affair and how your spouse reacts that will impact the children. (I assume that you would never flaunt an affair; *there is never a valid reason to do so.*) We will discuss the obvious, but unpleasant subject of Dealing With Discovery in greater detail later on in Chapter 24.

In summary, being the best parent or spouse you can be and fighting off the impulse to leave, so that your children have the security and influence of two parents under one moderately tranquil roof, may be an important reason to seek physical and emotional sustenance in the intimate company of a lover. Your sacrifice will be less painful and you will also be a better person to those around you, because you will have no cause to assume the obnoxious and self-destructive mantle of martyrdom.

2. Protecting the Physically Ill or Impaired Spouse

'... in sickness and in health...' Unless you or your spouse were either professional athletes or had physical problems of which you were both aware when you got married, this line from your vows was most likely the furthest thing from your mind. You have probably learned a bit about the frailty of human flesh since then.

Medical calamities occur in bad marriages, as well as good ones, and, given the nature of the discussion, let's deal with those first. The point I would like to make regarding illness arriving at the doorstep of a troubled relationship is distilled in this sad and funny joke:

Having thoroughly examined a middle-aged man, the doctor sent him back out into the waiting room and called his wife in to talk to her privately.

'The stress in your husband's life has taken a terrible toll on him,' said the doctor. *'Unless some major changes in his environment are made, I wouldn't bet on him living more than half a year. I strongly suggest that you try to make his home life as warm, loving and stress-free as possible. Be affectionate. Make him his favourite meals. Take an interest in his hobbies. Tell him how much he means to you. It will make all the difference in the world.'*

The wife nodded, got up and returned to the waiting room.

'What did the doctor say?' asked the husband.

'You'll be dead within six months,' she replied.

Modern, high-technology medicine is truly a miracle. It has raised both our hopes and expectations for long, vigorous and pain-free lives. When big problems arise, however, it can come at a staggering financial cost. The financial strain of a chronic illness on top of a divorce, (even an amicable one if it involves creating two households and only one spouse is well-paid), can wipe out the emotional well-being and financial security of both partners and any children, as well.

If there has been little communication in the marriage and one party, especially the stricken spouse, hasn't a clue that a divorce would have been imminent but for the illness, it may be more than a little difficult to have the long-overdue discussion now. Going to see a counsellor together, especially to discuss feelings about handling the illness, may save a lot of heartache and even the marriage itself. It will give you a chance to see your spouse in a new light and either surprise you or affirm your assessments of your spouse and marriage. If you feel that the financial and ethical responsibilities are such that you and your spouse are stuck together, you will have to assess how open you can be with each other about your needs and hopes (other than for a return to health). Although it is a rare occurrence and requires two exceptionally mature people, it may be possible that a 'marriage of convenience' can be worked out, with both parties agreeing on civil behaviour and a detailed financial plan. In such an event, discretion, rather than stealth, in the conduct of the extramarital relationship is what will be foremost.

Far more likely, however, will be an environment where the emotions are running far too high for such rational behaviour. Far worse than being under the same roof for the sake of the children you love is being locked together by sad events. It is a garden in which bitterness blooms.

Just as often, however, one partner in a decent marriage is visited by a tragic infirmity and becomes chronically, and perhaps fatally, ill. The other partner devotes a great portion of their life energy to caring for the sick spouse, and that burden, coupled with the loss of many of the attributes that made the marriage work, raises a dilemma for the caregiver as to how to meet the need for both spousal care and self-survival. Only those who have experienced it can know how truly draining it can be.

Anne, 41, married twenty years, one grown-up child, now a well spouse to a husband with ALS: *I've needed someone to comfort me and only me, somebody to ask about my day and to care that I might be stressed or overworked. The husband of a good friend of mine came by to do some of the odd jobs that had been backing up around the house. I guess it was his tenderness. I liked that he would ask if there was anything he could do for me. It all came tumbling out. I was so happy that weekend and so carefree. I actually could do whatever I wanted and eat whenever I wanted. I was focusing on life and pleasure instead of death and sickness. I thought it would just be a weekend fling, but when I came back I found myself constantly fantasising about it and him. Why can't I just have more of that? I want to discuss it with my husband, but I'm afraid that it will hurt him. I know marriage isn't all about physical stuff, but we used to have such a great sexual relationship and I am saddened by its loss. I want to be with him and take care of him, but I am afraid that, without my lover, I will just get more angry and resentful as time passes and my job gets bigger and bigger.*

Both partners deserve to find relief under such trying circumstances; if there are years of struggle or sacrifice ahead, you will need support from all quarters to be the best spouse you can be – either as uncomplaining patient or as patient caregiver.

3. Protecting the Children and Family Finances from a Spouse with Psychological Disorders or Mild Mental Instability.

We're not talking Daffy Duck here. You and the children shouldn't stay in the same house with anyone who threatens you with a knife or pops balloons behind the kids' heads to 'check their reflexes'. We're talking more along the lines of people who are not easily subject to control via drugs or have a poor prognosis from counselling, i.e. they can't really be improved by a pill or a therapist. (Any shrink worth his or her salt will admit that they can't do much with, for example, personality disorders.) These people are not crazy. They can separate reality from fantasy and function well enough to get custody of the children if they are likely to be more often available. So how did you get into this mess? Unless you're trained to look for it, people with these problems are often hard to spot. We meet them when we're young and our hormones are raging. They seem, on the surface, to be interesting and self-confident. If they're smart, physically attractive or both, we probably didn't stand a chance.

The practical problem with having a spouse of this sort is that he or she is generally not able to hold a job for very long (although when they're shown the door, it never seems to be their fault) and comfortably falls into the role of being your most needy dependant as well as your greatest critic. Why not divorce promptly? First, because you're the spouse who's working one and possibly two jobs to support the family, there's no way you'll get custody of the kids if it means that they will become 'latchkey' children. (Since you can't prove that your spouse has anything wrong with him or her other than a wretched personality, you won't make much progress on that front. In court, their acting will be masterful.) Second, your kids will need you more than they can admit (because your spouse would brand them as disloyal) and, third, unless they're pretty strong, independent and in their last years at home, when your divorce plans are announced, they will surely be drafted by your spouse into battle against you as scouts, envoys and B-52 pilots.

Of course, your spouse's emotional illness doesn't require a nasty edge to cause you to seriously review the affair option.

Kevin M., married 22 years: *My wife and I have been together many years and have two children (nine and twelve). When we were first together, it was great. My wife is very attractive and a nice person as well. But there has always been a certain sadness about her. Over the past twenty-plus years, circumstance and time have made her grow cold to me. We've been to counselling and have divorced once (before kids) and separated two years ago. She was diagnosed as co-dependent and depressed. She is on medication that buffers her sex drive and makes her gain weight. I love my kids and I know for a fact that they would be affected if I was not there to be with them; it was one of the things I learned when we were separated. It is very difficult now to live with someone who is unresponsive to you. I'm an interesting and good-looking guy who is in a bad situation. I'm not sure what to do. I can't leave because of the kids, but I find the thought of waiting until they're on their own to make a decision to leave my wife almost unbearable.*

This is also the time in your life when you are probably trying to save as much money as possible to send your child or children to the college or university of their choice. Costly divorce proceedings might well force your children to either assume a burden of debt that will be decades in the repayment process or attend the local community college, not only limiting their career choices and aspirations, but also depriving them of what may well be one of the richest and most crucial experiences in their personal development.

Again, a loving, clandestine relationship until the kids are accepted to their chosen institution (in which case you can point to money being earmarked and segregated for their use) can help you through the long wait until the exit door opens. This is one situation, however, where you will really need to look carefully at Chapters 9 and 15. You will honestly have to appraise your ability to carry off the subterfuge if you are married to someone who is innately suspicious and who will be indefatigable in his or her vindictiveness if you are found out.

SECTION B

Planning and Preparation for the
Adventure Ahead

CHAPTER 8

Getting Ready to Meet that Special Someone: Preparing Your Life, Preparing Yourself

You've taken that long, hard look at yourself, your spouse, your marriage and your life. You have reached some tough conclusions:

1. Whatever connection you had with your spouse that first brought the two of you together is irretrievably gone.
2. You have significant practical and moral commitments which you must, in good conscience, keep.
3. For reasons which you have carefully assessed and validated, divorce or separation is not an option for the next few years.
4. You will need the kind of joy and intimacy that only a lover can bring to enable you to be the best person you can for yourself and those you love, until a split from your spouse is possible.

Get ready. If you have the courage, determination and discipline that it takes, your life may be about to take a radical change for the better.

OK. So what happens now? You are probably asking yourself: *'Can I do this? Am I really going to be able to pull this off?'* After all, most of us aren't sociopaths. James Bond can kill a dozen people in a 24-hour period, including a beautiful woman he has just slept with, tell five different lies to ten different people and keep them all straight and have no trouble sleeping. That's neither normal nor healthy. We have consciences that give little signals that tell on us in many ways. (Indeed, con men look for these signals of vulnerability in their victims and refer to such a signal as a 'tell'. A great little film on the subject is *House of Games* starring Lindsay Crouse and Joe Montagna.) What's telling behaviour? Carly Simon put a long list in her song *'It's Not Like Him'*:

- hair combed at the end of the day
- clean and neat clothes
- hip sunglasses and boots
- politeness, smiling out of context
- putting on cologne
- eating oat bran, protein shakes and fruit smoothies
- having new interests in wine, poetry, zen, tennis and karate.

This isn't just a garden variety catalogue of a 'tell', it's a sledgehammer. What makes the song all the more poignant is that, as the 'wronged' woman feels her own grief, she sees something she has perhaps always wanted: her spouse's increased happiness, self-confidence and self-fulfilment. It should serve as a reminder to us, men and women alike, that this is a serious matter. We are not to take this as lightly as the man in the song so obviously does.

To be able to answer the 'Can I do this?' question honestly, you are going to have to discover a bit about yourself. It would be unrealistic of you to expect that you could make a major life change and not cause the slightest ripple in your most immediate relationships. The good part is, you don't have to; but you *will* need to learn the extent to which you give off telling behaviour signals and your ability to minimise and camouflage that telling behaviour. Obviously, the best time to find out whether you are telling anything is when you've got nothing to tell. Better to find out *before* you go bonkers over someone that you couldn't keep it a secret if you tried.

If we're going to be at all scientific about this, for starters, we'll need a kind of behaviour baseline, so that you can measure how things change in others' reactions to you as you change your schedule, activities and temperament. The first thing we are going to need to analyse is *time*. I don't have to tell you what you already know all too well – when you are in a bad relationship, you become keenly aware of its passage and of the waste you feel in your life. Let's do something about it. Having read this far, we should assume that you are at least somewhat inclined. What opportunity you have to follow up on that inclination will be, in large measure, the amount of time you have away from your spouse when you will not be very reachable or accountable.

Step 1: Get a small, spiral-bound notepad and, for at least a week, write down all of your activities.

Ordinarily one might suggest that you choose a week that is as typical as possible. How predictable are you? Could someone set a watch by the time you leave work for home or place a safe bet on what TV shows you'll watch each night? If you do vary your patterns, how much fluctuation is there? Naturally, if your life already swings wildly, it'll be pretty hard to pick up an occasional extra drum beat. Even if this week doesn't look like it will shape up to be typical, start *now*, anyway. You've wasted enough time already.

Strange as it may seem to some people, being married does not impose a duty to share with your spouse your every waking thought and get their approval before you can think the thought some more.[10] Indeed, that type of 'honesty' is about the most destructive behaviour I can think of. This time diary is also the first critical step towards re-establishing some kind of private life and will help with charting your surreptitious behaviour baseline (SBB, if we want to start using jargon!). Try writing your data in the diary in a personal code. Practise writing in the diary during private moments and hiding it in different places. Most of all, be accurate.

Step 2: Analyse how you spent your time.

You have 168 hours each week to account for. You will need several categories and subcategories *for each day*. The following

10 A fellow I know told me once that he had been out shopping at the supermarket with his wife. He picked up a Cosmo while waiting in the checkout queue and started reading an article titled something like '10 Great Sex Tricks to Thrill Your Man'. His wife snatched the magazine out of his hands and said 'You're disgusting.' 'What did I do?' he asked. 'With a perfectly straight face she replied, 'You're a thought criminal; that's enough.' Needless to say, they are no longer married.

outline, although by no means comprehensive, has been provided as a guide, and no one person would be expected to have an entry in every subcategory:

1. Time spent in proximity to your spouse:
A. unconscious (same or separate bedrooms)
i.   you sleeping or passed out.
ii. spouse sleeping or passed out.
iii. both sleeping or passed out

B. conscious, joint activities –
i.   eating
ii.   household chores
iii. attending to children
iv.   watching television
v.   shared reading or hobby
vi.   talking to each other or jointly telephoning others
vii. entertaining guests, family, business associates
viii. going out by yourselves for recreation
ix.   going out with friends or family for recreation
x.   going out by yourselves to do errands
xi.   going out with family or friends to do errands
xii. commuting
xiii. shared or commonly located work
xiv. sex

C. conscious, separate activities
i.   eating
ii. household chores

iii. attending to children

iv. watching television

v. reading, studying or hobby

vi. talking on the telephone

vii. entertaining guests, family

viii. doing work from the office

ix. playing computer games or Internet surfing

x. personal hygiene, bathroom

xi. sex (masturbation, of course)

2. Time spent away from your spouse:

A. In town

i. eating

ii. household chores

iii. attending to children

iv. watching television, playing on computer, or Internet surfing

v. school, studying, research

vi. talking to spouse on telephone (duration and number of calls)

vii. entertaining guests, family

viii. going out by yourself for recreation, hobby

ix. going out with friends, business associates or family for recreation

x. going out by yourself to do errands

xi. going out with family or friends to do errands

xii. commuting

xiii. work

xiv. business entertaining

B. On the road

i.   eating
ii.   in transit and checking into hotel
iii. business meetings
iv.   studying, research
v.   talking to spouse on telephone (duration and number of calls)
vi.   business entertaining
vii. going out by yourself for recreation
viii. going out with friends, business associates or family for recreation
ix.   going out by yourself to do errands
x.   bathroom, hygiene
xi.   sex (again, masturbation. If you're doing something else, I can't imagine why you are bothering with this time study)

What did you learn? You may be struck by how inefficient your seemingly busy life is. How many activities that are truly optional are being done out of habit or a warped sense of duty rather than pleasure? It's easy to by tyrannised by 'obligations' if you allow it.

Step 3. Analyse your data to extract a figure for how much time you and your spouse are away from each other, during which time there is no accounting for your whereabouts or activities. Are they many or few and far between? If you are a stay-at-home spouse without children under the age of four, you probably had a fair amount of unaccounted-for time during the week. The same is also true if you have developed a wide circle of friends and activities that you are pursuing by yourself: a charity, hobby club or the like. You may, on the other hand, look at your chart and weep: virtually every moment not devoted to work is spent in some odious familial obligation. The most common one: dragging the kids to a relative's house for an all-day visit. If that's the case, you're going to need to take positive steps to get a life, even if you decide eventually that you need a break from your routine more than you need a paramour. Wherever you fall in this continuum, at least now you have a baseline from which to start.

Step 4: Assess how well you carried off your surreptitious behaviour.

This is going to be a bit harder to quantify. I suppose that on a scale from 1 to 10, if your spouse found the notebook and asked what it was and you turned red as a beetroot and tearfully replied that you were taking a test to see how well you could handle a secret extramarital affair, you'd deserve a score of zero. Let's start out at the other end of the spectrum.

Did you do a fairly good job of tracking your activities? If you coded it, did you get adept at the encryption process? Did your book stay hidden? Did the week go by without your getting any indication that your spouse thought that there had been a change in you? If you answered yes to each question, give yourself a 10. Congratulations!

Did your spouse see you writing in your notebook? What did you say? Were you quick and said something like 'The company had a speaker in talking to us about time management and we were asked to try out some of his ideas' or 'I'm taking a quiz from a magazine I saw in the supermarket at the checkout?' If the rest of the week proceeded without any further comment from your spouse, give yourself a 9. Why so high, when you blew your cover? Because, no matter how careful you are, there will be a time when you will need to dissemble and this time you did it well. Do it as little as possible, for reasons which are obvious: the fewer false statements you make, the fewer you will have to keep track of.

If you did a pretty lame job of tracking your time in your diary, but your spouse didn't notice any oddness in your behaviour, you get an 8. Even though you didn't follow the assignment as well as you should have, you did change your behaviour without drawing attention to yourself. You will need to be more disciplined in the future. You should repeat the exercise for another week before moving on to the next step.

Below an 8, we begin to run into some real problems that will need fixing before we can go much further. Did the mere act of starting this 'habit diary' cause your spouse to indicate to you that your behaviour had changed? If you were able to keep track of your time and keep the recordkeeping secret, but your spouse commented that you seemed to be behaving strangely and you had no credible excuse (e.g. 'I don't know what you are talking about'), give yourself a 6.

Whether or not you got caught making notes, if you and your spouse got into an argument, ostensibly based on your behaviour, with accusation and denial, counter-accusation, etc., give yourself a 5 or lower depending on whether this was a run-of-the-mill fight or something special. The more out of the ordinary the confrontation, the lower your score; you were sending out extraordinary 'tell' signals and didn't handle the conflict too well. And, remember, you hadn't even done anything yet.

Even if you did not score very well, cheer up! If the fight was run of the mill, it will get lost in all of the others. If the fight was unusual, wait a few weeks and try again either with the same diary technique or with some of the ideas that follow. Besides, you've learned something about yourself *and* your spouse. Having tried this exercise, even though it didn't end well, will, I guarantee, cause you to give out fewer 'tells' the next time around.

Step 5: Look at your time diary and see where the opportunities for more private time may lie.

Some opportunities are not as promising as they may appear; for example, a job that keeps you running from one site to another all day. Sure you're out-of-pocket, but let's face it, there's a right time to fulfil your worklife requirements and a right time to handle your emotional needs. It's a common temptation to jeopardise the former for the latter. You'll have plenty of other temptations to deal with soon, so don't succumb to this one. Furthermore, worrying about one's career or financial situation in the midst of an affair that may be the cause of such worries is, to say the least, unsexy.

What about the other 100-plus hours each week when you're not at work? If you regularly take long solo bicycle rides or hike in the woods and paint watercolours on the weekends, you also have an obvious foundation of private time to build on. Ditto, if you are responsible for running errands, chauffeuring the kids, etc. I know you're thinking: But I've got a mobile phone and a pager and I can always be reached. We'll talk about the problem of the electronic leash and various strategies for freeing yourself later on in Chapters 15 and 16. For right now, as they say in New York, 'Fuhgeddaboudit.'

Step 6: Subtly restructure your life to increase the time available for solo activities.

Now is the time to do it, before you have anything to hide. You may wish, out of an abundance of caution to make the changes in stages, so that you can gauge what kind of and how much, if any, feedback you are getting from your spouse and children during the process, so that you can tweak your planning as necessary. As a start, review your diary to see where your household chores, which are usually done when the two of you are working together, could be done by taking time alone.

For example, let's say your Saturday morning ritual is to do the laundry while your spouse cleans the house. Do the laundry during the week instead of sitting with your spouse to watch his or her favourite television shows, which you may not even particularly care for. Don't announce that you're going to do the laundry; just start doing it. It may be a while before it even registers in your spouse's consciousness. (Television, by the way, is often used as a substitute for real life. You can live with less of it than you imagine and now is probably the best time to start. After all, remember that your goal is to have a secret, romantic liaison with an actual, attractive, real human being.) Obviously, on the day you decide to do this, don't announce that you're exhausted, etc. If you're doing a chore early, you're supposed to be chipper. If your spouse comments about your odd behaviour, make some denigrating comment about the show and say something like 'Well as long as I'm in the mood or I've got the energy to do it, I might as well take advantage of it.' *Do not say*: 'I've got some things I want to do on Saturday and I want to leave the morning free.'

When Saturday rolls around, have a personal errand to run. Be ready to have a real and legitimate answer if queried. Ask if your spouse needs you to do or get anything while you're out. It may even be wise, depending on where your spouse thinks your relationship is, to ask your spouse to join you (which, of course, screws up the routine). Return home within a period of time that could reasonably be expected, given the errands undertaken. You have now accomplished three goals: first, you have altered expectations as to what constitutes 'normal behaviour' for two different days; second, you have spent more time alone; and, third, you have created an expectation of a less orderly life, in general. While these may seem like trivial steps, they are the foundation of your affair, which, like the foundation under a building, is unseen but absolutely essential.

With respect to family obligations, if your spouse insists that it will kill his or her parents, aunts, uncles, cousins, etc. if you don't go every week, then say that you are going to use the time more constructively, either in work or recreation and that the spouse can go without you.[11] Then, do it. (Ironically, the reverse

---

11 This is not being rude or heartless. It is preventing exploitation. I greatly enjoy being with my grown children; they call me often and I get real satisfaction in hearing my twenty-something son and daughter say, 'I love you Dad,' when they hang up the phone. I know it's sincere. I would get no pleasure in trying to force them to visit me on some fixed schedule, whether I lived across town or across the country. It is sinful, in my opinion, for parents to blackmail their children with either guilt or threats to visit them.

also works. If your spouse doesn't want to accompany you to your parents' home, then he or she will surely not call you there very often. This will certainly give you more time if you leave your parents' early.)

If you are comfortable doing it, keep going with the time diary and chart your progress in creating more free time. You will be heartened by your progress, because you know you are building towards something truly rewarding.

Step 7. Building a 'love nestegg'.

While you are putting time aside for your affair, you should be putting money aside, too. Don't worry; this isn't like saving for college. You *will* have expenses, though, and they shouldn't be readily noticeable as larger than usual withdrawals and lower balances in the accounts you keep jointly with your spouse. If you feel that you cannot find a secure place to hide cash, get a post office box and use it as the address on a simple savings account that you keep at a bank where neither you nor your spouse do business. You won't want a cheque book (too much of a paper trail), just a cashpoint card.

How much will I need to save? Since you haven't met your love yet, you can't be certain, but in any event, like saving for a house or college, making a *regular* deposit matters most. Where will the money come from? From you, of course. Your spouse should not be aware of its absence. Neither, for reasons we'll discuss later, should your family incur any financial diminution on account of it. Most of us waste money on little luxuries and foolish choices every day. Yet, the pleasure of those luxuries will pale in comparison to the profound joy of being in the arms of your lover. Having a successful extramarital affair takes *discipline*. And there's no time like the present to begin practising it on every level. Depending on your circumstances, you should be able to save at least five and perhaps as much as twenty pounds per week.

Do you go to McDonald's or Starbucks for your second coffee and a second mini-breakfast or doughnut on your way to work? If you must have that hit of java, brew extra coffee at home and bring it with you, skip the doughnut and pocket the savings. If you're a typical person, you spend a fair amount on prepared foods, most of them, as you probably know, not very good for you. As we'll discuss, there's a lot of money to be saved here. Not only will you be building up your love nestegg (far healthier than an Egg McMuffin), but you will achieve some of the other goals you will set for yourself.

Do you buy a magazine or newspaper? You don't need to – after all, you're on the way to getting your own life and you will soon be less interested in vicariously living the glamorous lives of others. Besides, someone else in your office may have already bought one which you can read later on. You may need the *Financial Times* or some other publication as a business survival tool. Go ahead. You'll save elsewhere. But, if you feel you need to read certain publications in order for people to find you interesting, you aren't in the company of true friends and you're wasting your time. Remember to move the money you save each day to a separate place to be squirrelled away later.

Food and drink vending machines at work are another bad habit. Every time you go to the machine, you should look at your current temptation and note its cost. Take that exact amount of change and, while holding it in your hand, imagine an incredibly intimate moment with your paramour-to-be. Pretty nice, huh? Put the money back in your wallet, purse or pocket because, I promise you, it will bring your fantasy one step closer to reality each time you do.

Lunch. Ideally, you should bring a packed lunch, but this may be such a great change in your behaviour, that it will raise a zillion red flags, especially if your usual routine is to chow down at a cheap French bistro or the local steakhouse. Break out of your routine and try new and cheaper restaurants. If you go to lunch with co-workers, they may even appreciate the variety. When you do go, you won't have to order your 'usual' and can get something a little smaller or less expensive.

It should go without saying that frequenting an 'all-you-can-eat' restaurant is a bad idea. First, it's priced to make a profit on people who are expected to have big appetites, so that you have to gorge yourself on mediocre food to 'get your money's worth'. Second, eating like that is bad for your health in more ways than you want to hear about and will not make you a more attractive package to show the world. Finally, don't try to go there and order something from the menu. Even though it may sound logical, you will find yourself gazing longingly at the buffet and thinking, For an extra two-fifty, I could have eaten all that I want. You'll be setting yourself up for failure the following day and you will be no closer to embracing the love of your life.

If you eat at a company cafeteria or snack shop, tone down your purchasing a bit at a time. You may feel more hungry than usual at first, but keep the vision of your impending affair foremost in mind; you will draw comfort from it and the sense of deprivation will subside. You may even find, to your own surprise, that you are more animated and outgoing with friends and colleagues than usual.

Sundry purchases. It's amazing how much more expensive name-brand items are than their generic equivalents. It is now possible to compare food and drug ingredients, strengths, calories, nutrients, cost per unit, etc on the labels of goods. You may even occasionally discover that the shelf brands are not only lots cheaper than the nationally advertised ones, but more nutritious, as well. There's no need to impress the cashier at the checkout counter with your profligacy. Pocket the difference.

Although it may seem hard not to make an exception, this also applies to items that you may even have a strong emotional attachment to or reliance upon. It especially affects purchases that you may think are necessary as part of your new plans. In my experience, this applies more often to women than men and I have tailored my comments accordingly.

If you go into any department store, you will notice that the first place you hit is the cosmetics counter. It takes up maybe 10% of the store's space but provides ninety percent of the profits because the mark ups are so huge. Although it may give *you* a lift to get the latest shade of lipstick, do not think that you're doing it for a guy. Approximately 10% of white males generally have some form of colour blindness. It's hardly surprising then that most men cannot tell the difference between a gloss that came from Tesco and one that came from Elizabeth Arden. Instead of buying the latest champagne-mocha-taffy-frappé or other hip colour, put the cash aside and imagine buying your lover some cute little memento. (Lest you think I'm being one-sided or, worse yet, sexist here, I'll give a little personal aside: I'm going bald slowly enough for minoxidil to make a difference and I've got a real emotional attachment to what thinning hair I have left. For years, I dutifully got a prescription and shelled out £27 a month for Rogaine, an American treatment for hair re-growth. You might think that with so much riding on my decision and having been a loyal user for several years I would have had some hesitation. Nope. As soon as the patent expired and the generics appeared, I switched to a house brand, saving £65 a year.)

As far as other fashion accessories go, unless they're fetishists (and in which case you would not find them good bed partners), when a man looks at a woman, he does not notice the following unless they are weird, loud, large or garish: shoes, handbags, jewellery, belts and nail polish. If you're tempted to spend money on these items to enhance your attractiveness, don't. Put the money in the love nestegg instead. What expenditures then *are* good investment bets? Hey, we're trying *not* to spend money here! But if you insist and you can do it without arousing the spousal antennae, here's what I recommend for women: Clothes and hairstyle that project a softness, openness and self-assured/independent streak. Neither slutty, schoolmarmish, too tailored nor high-tech/haute couture. A man *will* notice the length of a skirt, the neckline of a top and the texture and sheen of a dress, sweater or blouse. They may even be more memorable to him than the colour of the garment itself. Women with killer figures who bop around all day in tight-leg jeans and silk blouses obviously don't need my advice on how to get men's attention, except to be told that, despite being luscious, you may unintentionally project a look that is a bit too dangerous for a clandestine relationship. When a guy is betting his physical, financial and emotional health, he tends to be more cautious than when he was single. We'll discuss this some more later on in Chapter 9.

For men the job is somewhat easier, because, in general, women are more accepting, have more widely varying tastes and fewer stereotypical fantasies. Wear the kind of clothes that you're comfortable in (they will tell women, who are generally more observant than men, a lot about you and provide a sort of 'opening conversation'), but try being just a tad cleaner and neater than usual. The powers of observation in women, being so well developed, also mean that buying clothing out of your usual style will alert your wife. A final note for both men and women: start cutting back on the fragrances until you're using practically none at all; let yourself run out and don't repurchase it. Perfume and cologne can be picked up by others long after the wearer is desensitised to it and you and your lover will want to protect each other from suspicion. Remember the Carly Simon song mentioned earlier? Smell is a powerful stimulus only when it is linked to memory. All of the glossy, innuendo-filled advertising notwithstanding, you won't attract potential lovers with it, unless it reminds them of someone else. That is probably not the effect you intend. Once your affair gets going, you can revisit the perfume/cologne issue. We'll discuss it further in Chapters 16 and 19.

There are a number of books on simplifying your life; they're pretty useful and provide many more tips on managing your money and how to live more frugally. Look through a few when you're at the library. You get the idea: think cheap, not for cheapness' sake, but for the warm glow and touch of excitement you will get from knowing that each pound saved will pay you back a thousandfold!

What will the money be for? Unless there is a great disparity in incomes between you and your future love, you will probably be sharing the costs of hotel rooms, dinners, bottles of champagne, little gifts, taxis, extra petrol, etc. You should be prepared. Your affair is going to be an intimate *relationship*; it is not a 1950's-style one-time date where the rule is simply 'the guy pays'. Even if the man wants to foot the entire cost, the woman may wish, for her own sense of dignity and commitment, to share the cost, at least for her own taxis, petrol, etc. Both should be ready for either alternative. There are other benefits to putting money away in this fashion which will be discussed in later chapters.

Step 8. Feeling Better About Yourself.

This is going to be trickier than you might imagine, because this is the time when the 'tells' will begin to sprout. A French dramatist once said, 'The most difficult secret for a man to keep is the opinion he has of himself.' If you have successfully started building more private time into your life and begun growing your love nestegg, you're probably in a better mood already. Has your spouse noticed? Being nicer to your spouse is often the first sign that something's cooking. If it causes your spouse to be more pleasant in return, there is no *immediate* problem. However, you shouldn't go overboard with giddiness and get sloppy. 'Success breeds success', but it can also breed arrogance. That's not you, is it?

If your upbeat mood is greeted with wariness and suspicion, you will need to be more aware of yourself. You may be surprised to discover how your past demeanour reflected your anger and inner turmoil in so many ways. It's a shame, but, even though you shouldn't pick weird fights out of the blue, be aware that you may have to behave a little more poorly than you feel. If necessary, remind yourself that, if you weren't boxed in by all of the moral commitments that you have decided to keep, you wouldn't have to waste a part of your life going through the elaborate charade that you are now in the midst of.

You may have already begun to take the next important step, when you began saving on lunch and snack money. That's making yourself healthier and more attractive. The reasons are obvious; of course, you want someone to fall for you because you are a warm, loving and pleasing person to be with, but, in order to radiate those qualities, you will need to boost your own confidence. Once you do, you will have an added bonus: by enlarging the pool of those who may be attracted to you, you will know that you and your lover have actively chosen each other and that neither of you are merely 'settling for the best I can do'.

Are you at your proper weight and level of body tone? If you are, I congratulate you. You are in a happy minority and I don't just pass it off to your genetic inheritance; you have good health habits. Current PC vogue to the contrary, our society does *not* have an 'obsession with thinness'. As US author and obesity expert Michael Fumento noted in a guest editorial in the *Wall Street Journal*, 29 September, 1997: 'Americans are the fattest people on earth. A third of us are certifiably obese (more than

20% overweight), and about three-fourths are heavier than our optimal weight. We've gained an average of *twelve pounds* in just the last decade.' As numerous cover stories in weekly magazines appearing in the years since that story eloquently testify, it has only got worse. Although it's now politically correct to preach 'fat acceptance', it's bad health and bad social policy because obesity increases the cost for both chronic and acute medical care to individuals and society as a whole by a tremendous amount. Besides, making love is a physical and aesthetic experience as well as an expression of affection. You will enjoy it more if you feel more confident in your appearance, stamina and the sense of pleasure and admiration that you impart in your lover.

How do you get from A to B? There are hundreds of books at the major chains on living a healthier lifestyle. Assuming that you are not currently under a doctor's care for some particular condition that requires a special diet or exercise regimen, the entire collection of *legitimate* texts can be reduced to a few, simple and, at times, politically incorrect, guidelines. Why politically incorrect? Because some of the companies that have the warmest, fuzziest and hippest images are selling unhealthy stuff. Here then are the principles:

1. *Calories Do Count.* Sorry, but anyone who tells you otherwise is trying to get you to part with your money in exchange for a fantasy. When you buy prepared foods, *read the damn labels*!
2. *Eat as little fat as possible, especially saturated fat.* Beef, lamb, pork and all of their derivative products are loaded with fat. Chicken, turkey and fish are not only better for you, but also are

usually cheaper. Dairy products can also be a problem. If you like cheese, choose one with a strong flavour so that a little will go a longer way. A one-ounce cube of mild cheddar is smaller on one edge than a postage stamp, yet four of them will equal the calories of a burger with mayo on a bun. Butter, of course, is virtually solid fat. What about those really nice guys Ben & Jerry? Read their labels. They may be trying to save the rainforests, but they're not doing anything to help reduce coronary heart disease, stroke, diabetes and colon cancer. Frying foods, especially after covering them with some crispy batter mix – chicken, fish, potatoes, onion rings, etc. – obliterates the beneficial effects of substituting them for red meat in the first place. Potato and tortilla chips, pork rinds (I'm afraid to imagine *what* they're made of) and other snack foods take up entire aisles in the supermarket. Just read the labels. I won't rave any further.

3. *Eat more fibre.* Like Mum said, eat your fruits and vegetables. Have your sandwiches on wholewheat bread or rolls. Broccoli and sweet potatoes are great stuff. You may not care for broccoli at first. Eat it anyway, as if it's a medicine. After a while you will find that you've acquired a taste for it.

4 *Reduce your caffeine intake.* I know, you live for Starbucks and your Diet Coke. Try it for a week to see if you can do it. Put the money you save in your love nestegg and think about how this discipline will return you big dividends in the months ahead.

5. *Don't use tobacco.* Notice I'm not just talking cigarettes here. I mean the whole nine yards – cigars, pipes, snuff and chewing tobacco. I don't need to tell you the health reasons. Just look at it this way: by quitting, you will not only save money but also

greatly increase the number of people who are willing to consider being your lover. I don't care if the hip *du jour* are smoking cigars. It may work this month for Arnold Schwarzenegger and Demi Moore, but, believe me, it won't work for you. So why rule out otherwise nice people just because they don't want their first kiss to taste like licking an ashtray?

6. *Drink lots of water.* Water is good for you. It may be chic to carry a bottle of Evian, but it's not necessary to have a name brand. Keep a bottle with you, however, and drink from it often. If you have access to a company water cooler, great. Assuming the water supply where you live is up to snuff, tap water is also fine; otherwise buy the cheapest mountain spring water on the shelf.

7. *Walk more.* Rippling biceps may be nice and abs that you can bounce a coin off may likewise be appealing, but if you suddenly set yourself on a path designed to make you become a David Beckham or Nell McAndrew lookalike, the whole world, not only your spouse, will know that something's up. You don't need a health club, gym, fancy running outfits or other paraphernalia to get into reasonably good shape. Just comfortable shoes. First of all, walking is free. Second, it's non-obvious behaviour. There are opportunities to walk more all of the time: parking your car at the far end of the car park when shopping or going to work, walking to the restaurant on your lunch hour, using stairs instead of the lift, etc. And finally, the cardiovascular benefits are just as real as jogging and you will have less risk of injury.

8. *Meditate.* I'm not suggesting that you sit cross-legged on the floor, burn incense and hum 'Ohhhmmm' for half an hour

every day, even though it *is* a good idea. Stress takes a tremendous toll on the body and ages us physically, emotionally and spiritually. Your marriage may be your greatest source of stress right now and you need to find a calm refuge. Get into a regular habit of devoting just five minutes at a time to contemplation of some simple thing while trying to make the rest of your mind and sensations blank; it will work wonders.

9. *Seek moderation.* When enthusiasm strikes you, it's easy to overdo things. Don't. First, from a practical standpoint, radical behaviour changes are tells. Secondly, you can rapidly lose your enthusiasm because the change will appear too difficult if you try to accomplish it all at once. Finally, you will be balancing your home, work and love life in the future and, in maintaining that balance, moderation will be a necessity. Better to start practising now.

10. *The first nine are enough.* You don't need a nice round number (or the magical numbers 7 or 12) to have a logical list. OK, girls and boys, here comes the fun part.

CHAPTER 9

Finding, Evaluating and Choosing Your Lover

The Search

When you began reading the Introduction to this book, you may have thought that, by telling you that 'You are not alone', there was only an attempt being made to give you some cover or comfort. Maybe you thought that you were being offered the sheer company of numbers to ease your longing and distress. Not so. There is a great flip side to that introductory statement. Depending on the size of your community, there are hundreds, perhaps thousands of people of the opposite sex who are in a frame of mind to meet, flirt, court and make love with you. They have no expectations or demands to make of you other than that you love, respect and cherish their company. They do not seek marriage, money, status or the total commitment of your time and energy. They will not be consumed with jealousy if you sleep with your spouse, because they understand that that is part of your circumstances. They are, in short, much like yourself in needs, situation and outlook. All you need to do is to find each other.

Where do you begin? Statistically, the greatest number of affairs start at work. People are thrown together in close quarters for long periods of time; they share common goals and problems; their tasks are interdependent and often mutually supportive. They see each other at their best: well-dressed and competent. They learn about each other's tastes, preferences, hopes, concerns, sense of humour, capacity for empathy and the like. This is fertile soil for love to grow and blossom. Unfortunately, as I don't have to tell you, the soil can turn to quicksand almost without warning. Your co-workers will figure out your intimate relationship unless you are both supercool and subtle. Furthermore, just about everyone who is not in the midst of an affair of their own will be jealous. Jealously breeds gossip and a secret pleasure in seeing an affair end badly.

When enveloped in the thrall of love, it is difficult to see disaster looming. I will not go through a detailed analysis of each item in the litany of problems. Nevertheless, the possibilities for you to create a first-class fiasco are numerous: sexual harassment and discrimination claims from non-participants, potential sanctions from your employer or the government, discovery by the spouses and enough financial ruin, embarrassment and humiliation to go around for just about everyone connected to the liaison. Self-employed professionals will fare even worse: doctors and lawyers can lose the their livelihoods if they are so stupid (and they are!) as to sleep with a patient or client. The strongest recommendation I can make: *Don't do it*. You *can* find your special someone without resorting to adding an extra level of danger to your situation. If the idea of the danger factor excites you, better think twice about going forward unless you also have a happy fantasy of wallowing in the sticky mess you will probably create.

What if, in spite of it all, you *do* fall mutually in love with someone at work? If possible, you should both consider finding new employment at different companies, so that neither of you is subject to the scrutiny of co-workers. If that is not possible, at least one of you should leave (if you're a professional, end the professional relationship and refer your potential lover to another service provider *before* you consummate your desire for each other) and you should immediately have a heart-to-heart talk about your long-term goals for the relationship and be sure that you are in complete agreement; you will not only need to establish strict ground rules for your behaviour as you would in any affair, you will also need to spell out for and with each other what you are willing to risk and lose so that any later recriminations and bitterness will be kept to a minimum. Much of what we'll be discussing later on in Chapter 17 will apply here.

Your friends and neighbours are likewise out of bounds. First of all, they're probably not who you're really looking for; they're just a reflection of that old 'grass is always greener...' feeling. With friends, it can happen when you go out with another couple and get loose and start having fun together. Or maybe it was someone you dated and even may have slept with, about whom you now have regrets for not having married. 'If only...' is an extremely wobbly basis for a relationship, since, more often than not, you would discover that your present spouse was probably the better of two poor choices you made when you were young. With neighbours, an attraction is often just a fantasy spun out of your own imagination as you watch them do their outside chores in some graceful or endearing manner or, more blatantly, you secretly ogle them as they do their stretches before they go off jogging. Although this is only the second most common way that affairs begin, it is also one of the biggest, stickiest messes you can make.

Another all-too-common category is virtually *always* such a colossal disaster that it almost doesn't bear mentioning. Unless, of course, you're watching Trisha, Jerry Springer or God knows who else. People actually sleep with their in-laws: fathers, mothers, brothers, sisters, sons and daughters. Ugh! OK, so you dated your husband's or wife's younger brother or sister before you got married. Sorry, guys and gals, it's too late to make the Young Rascals' 'Did You Ever Have To Make Up Your Mind?' your theme song.

Just because the most convenient, accessible and intimately known people in your life are off-limits, does not mean that you have to proposition people on street corners. You will be surprised how many lives intersect with your own every day. Indeed, there's a play called *Six Degrees of Separation* whose title is derived from the surprising fact that everyone knows everyone else in the world via a chain of six or fewer people. You will meet people casually through other people who would never imagine that they may be introducing two future lovers to each other. Awareness, persistence and openness will be what counts most.

Before you even start looking, however, you must follow certain rules for your own ethical behaviour.

1. First of all and probably the most difficult at the outset: *Never pretend that you aren't married.* You are not looking to deceive someone into falling in love with you and then breaking the news to them. You've got one major deception going in your life already and that is quite enough. Besides, you *want* a lover who will be understanding and discreet. Nine times out of ten, they, too, will be married. After lying to them, you cannot expect real intimacy or loyalty to your needs, especially when family obligations and the needs of your lover conflict. If you have a wedding ring that you usually wear, keep it on; there are lots of ways you will be able to send signals that it's not one you rejoice in. By the way, ladies, if you have a large diamond engagement ring, you might consider wearing it less often; not only is it a magnet for thieves, but it sends out a subtle message that you expect to be well taken care of and that you may have a rich and powerful husband. Even if nothing is further from the truth, it's not inviting for a man to have the thought briefly flash through his mind: 'Great; I sleep with this woman and, not only will it bankrupt me, I get my legs broken.'

2. *Be honest and matter-of-fact about your circumstances.* This is more subtle, because there is a natural tendency to gild the lily and play the martyr. Your husband doesn't have to beat you and your wife doesn't have to be an alcoholic for someone to feel that you are not a bucket of slime for seeking an extramarital relationship. We all know how complex and conflicting life is and we play the cards of circumstance that we're dealt to the best of our ability and with the best of intentions. Don't anticipate being judged harshly and you won't be. Your lover-to-be is not

about to give you the same kind of hard time as your mother-in-law would.

3. *Don't lead someone on with the impression that they might become your lover, in order to satisfy other short-term needs of your own, after you have already decided that they aren't 'the One'.* This rule and the one that follows are really important. In a bad marriage, time is always a constant enemy. You wouldn't want someone to waste yours. Don't waste theirs. If you are only interested in this person as a friend, ally or a shoulder to cry on, say so, even if it takes the most graphic terms. To hold out hope to a person that there will be romance and physical intimacy where there is no hope is cruel and you don't deserve their affection.

4. *Don't enter into an affair with the idea that it will be an 'interim' relationship until someone comes along that you find more appealing.* You and your lover already know that your relationship is most probably a temporary one and will end when one or the other is no longer married. Considering how the deep bonds created by an affair bring two souls so terribly close together, that's already going to be a lot to deal with. Each of you owes the other sincere, deep and respectful affection for as long as the affair lasts. We'll discuss this in greater detail later on in Chapter 17.

Very well then. How do you get to meet all of these people? Bars? Nyet! There may be singles bars, gay bars and sports bars, but there are no *safe* bars for married people looking for lovers. Ninety-nine times out of a hundred, unless you live in a big, anonymous city, such places are so well known that just having an acquaintance see your car there would start tongues wagging. Besides, going to a bar alone is rarely a promising romantic strategy for straights, single or married. And, if that's not enough, just remind yourself that this activity is not something you can do with your friends. Remember, you're not looking for a one night stand. You also want a high level of trust and a low chance of picking up some sexually transmitted disease.

Since we're speaking about danger, this is probably a good place to talk about meeting someone on the Internet via an activity that is sometimes called cybersex. (Here, I'm not talking about the kind of activity discussed earlier in Chapter 1 that stays limited to diddling one's keyboard and one's self.) I have heard lots of people say that they met someone in an Internet chat room, got to know them, eventually moved to sending e-mail back and forth, arranged a meeting and started an affair. An indication of how often such affairs occur is in the comment of one private investigator who estimates that 15% of his cases involve affairs that began in Internet chat rooms:

It's middle- age crazy. They get bored; they get a computer; they play solitaire and then go to chat rooms. The next thing you know, they're meeting someone at a Travelodge.

Sounds great? A few words of caution. The Internet is a notorious place for aliases and imagined personae. In front of our keyboards and screens, we are all Mel Gibsons and Gwyneth Paltrows. However, you don't want to end up playing the Michael Douglas or Diane Keaton role in your own personal version of the movies *Fatal Attraction* or *Looking for Mr Goodbar.* But, *if* you can spend home time in front of the computer without arousing suspicion and *if* your spouse isn't likely to become a competent hacker into your e-mail, this may be an avenue worth cautiously pursuing. (This is no longer as easy as it once was. In Chapter 14, we will discuss the current crop of truly intimidating spy software.) Tell your e-lover that you will be using an e-alias until you have met in person and have had a chance to reinforce your mutual attraction, trust and respect for each other. They should also appreciate how high the stakes are and will understand, especially if things don't work out at your first meeting, in which case you can part friends without worrying that someone out there knows that you're on the prowl and wants to blackmail you or perpetrate some other horror. Personally, I'd pass.

Let's look at more promising places in your current environment before we try to seek out new sites.

For the majority of us who drive to work every day, commuting is not a promising way to meet a potential lover. Driving by bus stops and offering strangers of the opposite sex a lift to town is an unlikely and dangerous way to make contacts; moreover, even if you aren't interrogated by the police, it's sure to earn you a kind of notoriety you'd rather avoid. Car and van poolers really fall into the category of friends and neighbours and carry with them the same potential problems. On the other hand, trains, trams and the Tube offer far greater possibilities for meeting people, and a good-natured response to the forced intimacy of a crowded carriage can yield many possibilities for finding out in a low-risk and low-key way if someone you find interesting is also interested in you. A smile accompanied by a simple 'May I sit here?' as you take a seat next to the person will provide an opening to gauge their friendliness. If you're reading different newspapers, you can offer to swap when you've both finished. These small indicators, easy to give and read with no direct indication of your designs, are a safe way to start. Another great aspect of a train is that the number of carriages gives you an opportunity to scope out a fair number of people and, if you do click with someone, it will be easy to begin your pre-affair courtship. If things don't work out, well, there's always a different carriage. For bus users, it can be more problematic because the timetables for a particular bus may not be as closely adhered to as a commuter train, but the principles are the same.

Is your workplace absolutely useless to you, merely because co-workers, suppliers and customers should be off-limits? Absolutely not. Companies often solicit the after-hours volunteer help of employees to work on community outreach projects, play on corporate league teams, assist with charity fundraising activities and the like. These can be genuine career builders, helping you rub shoulders with the company's VIP for whom the particular charity is a pet project. If you're on a corporate sports team, for example, there's often lots of camaraderie with opposing teams, the loser buying a round at the local pub, etc. It's not only a good way of networking and learning about what other opportunities in your industry or particular skill speciality may be around, but also a great way to meet other married people *sans spouses* in a low-pressure, friendly environment. A phone number may not only give you a line on a new job, but the names of other people who may share your interests and work background.

In many cities and suburban communities, couples often meet through their children's activities. In the days of the 1960s and 70s, wives had the traditional role of carting playmates back and forth between houses, to scout meetings and the like, and men were pretty much absent from the process; indeed, one of the wife's roles was to build the family's social life. A lot of that has changed, and mums and dads often share equally in handling the logistics of their kids' extramural lives. It's important for you to stay emotionally engaged with your children at all times, especially if the relationship with your spouse has been strained. If not properly handled, however, relationships with adults met through your children may often be too close to home for comfort. Children are very alert to emotional subtlety. When little Ashley blurts out that Mummy starts acting funny and laughing a lot every time Emily-Jane's daddy drops her off at the house, Mummy will not be thinking of recounting her daughter's remark at the next family party. Like contacts via the office, meeting people through your children should, ideally, be a 'once removed' process. But how do we do this?

Let's start with the clichéd involvement of parents in their kids' lives: sports and clubs. These are activities which you *should* be involved in. They will pay big dividends in your relationship with your children, regardless of whether they hold out the potential for meeting your new lover. But hold out potential they do. After-school football, netball or whatever sport your child is involved in not only bring competing teams together, but also often have field-sharing with several different age groups. If your schedule allows it, don't just attend games, volunteer to help out. There are many things you can do, even if you aren't knowledgeable enough to coach the kids (that's so time-consuming, by the way, that you would have no time at all to meet people). The coach may need an assistant in keeping track of the equipment, contacting other teams to change schedules or the like. Your child will appreciate your involvement and it's pretty hard for the spouse to object to such well-intentioned solo activity. After being around for a while, you will probably have a fair sense of how much your child is watching you and how much attention he or she needs. Their needs, obviously, come first. But, as the season wears on and the bonds of the team strengthen, there will be fewer glances over to the sidelines; you will soon feel almost superfluous. If you have a straightforward enough relationship with your child, you may ask, 'Do you mind if I walk around a bit or would you like me to stay right here?' Since your volunteer tasks have you interacting with grown-ups generally, the child will probably assume any distantly viewed activity of yours is some kind of official, grown-up business.

Although most of your contacts will be with parents of your child's teammates, you will, over time, get to know your 'opposite numbers' on other teams and parents you see repeatedly on the sidelines or in the car park, either because their children are on the opposing team or because they're there for another game being played nearby. Children, their joys and foibles are an easy topic of conversation and provide numerous avenues for discussions of domestic situations.

Scouting and its variants provides another fertile ground to meet people. Although being a leader can be time consuming and, at times, a ghastly torture, you can help out with ancillary work, such as getting supplies for the entire pack or troop, arranging meetings and so forth. The situations and possibilities here are similar to those described in the previous paragraphs and don't need to be spelled out again.

If your schedule conflicts with these activities, does it mean that there aren't things you can do with and for your child that will be both beneficial for him or her and increase your opportunity to meet that special someone? Absolutely not. Most public libraries are open late during the week. (Although I'm really tempted at this point to talk about what a great idea it is for its own sake to get your kids away from the television and into the library, I'll skip the lecture. Like changing your diet, it's one of those common-sense things that isn't always easy to do.) The library is a natural place and time for similarly situated adults to meet each other. Discussions about children's books, even if your kids are of different ages, is a natural opener to discussing a variety of books and issues that will lead to a conversation of one's marital status and intentions in a quiet, gentle and non-loaded way. It will also be a useful aspect, as we will discuss later, of evaluating the person as a potential lover.

What about the local Ottakers or Waterstones? Although the big chain bookshops are now more family-friendly and have the added comfy bonus of coffee bars, you may face the dilemma of having to purchase books that otherwise could have been borrowed. A book addict myself, I can see how this could get expensive. Depending on your circumstances, you could attract the attention or ire of your spouse. (Raiding your love nestegg is, of course, out of the question. After all, not only will it undo weeks' worth of scrimping, but what do you say when you're asked where you got the money?)

If you already belong to a health club, you may want to try

varying your hours. Most people have a regular schedule and you see them all the time. If you have friends or co-workers who work out when you do, it won't do to strike up a conversation with someone in their presence. If you followed the advice in the previous chapter, you have created more free time for yourself which you can now 'swap' with your regular workout time.

You've probably already had the experience of running errands and catching the eye of someone who you found appealing, but didn't have the nerve to follow it up. Maybe you weren't sure if they were sending out a vibe or just being friendly. This time you'll be more alert for it when it happens again. A big smile and a 'Hi, there!' crosses the line so gently that, if you're wrong, you can just say, 'Sorry, I didn't have my glasses on and you looked familiar.' The supermarket is a notorious meeting place for urban singles, but does it work for married people? Although I don't know of any studies on the subject, I'd say probably not. Supermarket cruising smacks a little bit of desperation (even if that's what you're feeling, it's not a sexy emotion to advertise). However, you *can* choose your checkout line and follow someone who may have met your meaningful glance with a smile earlier in your meanderings. Nothing starts up a conversation quicker than picking up a magazine at the checkout and laughing at headlines such as 'Princess Di's Will Leaves Fergie Secret UFO Sex Diet'.

The main problem with meeting people while on errands is the brevity of the contact; it seems at the time that there's little room for subtlety if the person is not to be lost forever. You can, if necessary, just give them a long glance and say, 'Hmm, it's 6.30 p.m. already and I've got to get going; I guess I'll have to come back here tomorrow at the same time.' If your romantic interest is indeed also interested, they may come back with a different time or place or may merely say, 'Maybe I'll see you then.' Odds are pretty good that, if you arrive five minutes early, they'll be there. If you have met a similarly situated married person, they will understand that there isn't a whole lot of time for shallow, cocktail party conversation as a prelude to serious talk. When your first 'date' after meeting rolls around, *then*, you can stroll down the aisles in a more leisurely fashion.

Undertaking new activities that take you out of the house may well constitute a telling change in your behaviour. If you gradually lay a foundation, such as by reading and commenting on local newspaper articles, flyers from school and the like, you will have a basis for expanding outside involvement: the local parent-teacher organisation offers possibilities, as do other types of after-school parental activity such as supervising children in building scenery for the school Christmas play. Also give some thought to civic involvement. If a particular local issue has been stuck in your craw, this might be a good time to get your community spirit revved up, as well as meet lots of people. Encourage your spouse to be the one to get active in the neighbourhood watch programme; that's too close to home for you and, if you stay with the kids, it will build up your right to equivalent outside time for your events. Your spouse may want to go, too, but, hey, someone's got to stay home with the kids and this time it's not your turn. Again, the key is to work these activities in gradually and with seeming spontaneity.

Is there a skill or interest that you have been wanting to develop or perhaps a gap in your education that you want to fill? The local community college, museum or other source of adult education programming is a likely place to meet other married people. The fact that they are taking classes means that they, too, want or have more direction than just cruising along in their status quo rut. Like you, they imagine or dream of a better or different life situation, and the sense of freedom to think and express ideas that comes from being on a college campus is infectious. Besides, it brings back memories of when you were back in school and fancy free – very sexy stuff, indeed.

When it comes to choosing your course subject matter, however, a word of caution: don't take courses in psychology or sexual matters, especially if you've never expressed an interest before. Way too loaded. First, your spouse will be *very* interested in what the class and your classmates are like and will examine your face for tells while demanding a high level of detail. Secondly, there's a 'physician-heal-thyself' syndrome: the kind of people such classes attract usually have unresolved problems of their own, some of which may be rather severe. These people can be dangerous and destructive if you let them get close to you. Classes which will attract a similar type may include spirituality, massage, astrology or anything else vaguely new agey. Hobbies can pose problems, too, because they tend to be highly sex-linked. A man doesn't take a course in automobile maintenance expecting to have a class that has many married women and a woman who chooses to learn the art of macramé won't find herself in the company of many straight men. Why not go against type? In addition to raising eyebrows at home, you may be the only man in a needlepoint class or the only woman in a model railroading course. Try explaining *that* to your spouse. Of course, you'll get lots of attention; so much so that you will become an object of interest and intrigue for the entire class. Far better to keep a lower profile. Highly technical classes may also be a bad choice for the opposite reason – too little human interaction. There's not much opportunity or inclination to chat when you're hunched over a keyboard trying to master the intricacies of a spreadsheet and graphics program. What's good? Didn't the liberal arts students always seem to be having the best times? Literature, art and music appreciation and drama are always good possibilities. Lots of discussion and interaction that's not overly self-focused is a good starting place to learn about your lover-to-be.

Every community, whether it's a major urban area, suburban patchwork or rural area has its particular traditions and activities. Look at yours and apply the above suggestions with care, thought and caution.

Evaluating Your Potential Lover

OK, so you've had a few conversations with that someone and the two of you seem to enjoy each other's conversation and physical proximity. Now what? Try to flirt, sweet talk and otherwise manoeuvre them into bed and see if the sex is good, too? Not quite. Unlike 'On Top Of Old Smoky', no one is going to accuse a person pursuing an extramarital affair of 'a-courtin' too slow'. Just getting to know your special someone has been a bold act. Now is really the time to stop and think about your choices. First of all, you have to realise that the criteria that you should apply when evaluating someone as a potential lover are very different from choosing a date, a weekend companion for a trip or a spouse. With the first, you want someone who won't embarrass you in front of your friends by getting drunk and throwing up all over you. With the second, you want someone who can scuba dive, laugh and dance all night and make love three times a day. And with the third, the list is really long. Long enough, in fact, that you obviously didn't get some critical items. If you'd been wiser, some of them might have been in your top half-dozen most-desired attributes.

Your initial reaction might be that the attributes you want in your lover are precisely those that are missing in your spouse. Not necessarily. Merely because your spouse may not be the outdoors type does not mean that your lover should be an avid backpacker and skier. The two of you will have little opportunity to share your enthusiasm for the hills and forests without arousing suspicion. Better to cultivate friends of your own sex who will share your interests. Similarly, if you want or have children, you would want a spouse who was long on patience and an enthusiastic participant in the parenting process. Your lover may have empathy and interest in your parental trials and tribulations, but whether the parental role suits *them* should not be a major issue for you. On a more intimate level, having a spouse who is boring and unenthusiastic in bed doesn't mean that you would want to choose for your paramour a sexual acrobat who would arrive at your assignation with a case full of adult toys.

What you want most at this time is someone with whom you can be happy to share your feelings, love, laughter and desire. Your lover should be your sanctuary and paradise to seek out, find contentment and luxuriate in. Those who are to become likely candidates will have to meet certain criteria if your affair is to survive, succeed and blossom. You cannot know the soul of another, but there are certain things that *you* must believe if you are to take the big step with this special person.

1. You must have a strong belief that they are emotionally stable, trustworthy, flexible and mature.

I don't have to tell you how great are the risks, how very much is at stake, when you start a clandestine affair. This is not a one-night stand you're planning. There are a lot of very sexy people who are also jealous, spiteful, showoff-y or just a little mad. And if things don't go their way, their natural reaction is going to be to look out for Number 1 and do whatever they feel furthers their own interests or sense of justice. You don't need to enter into a relationship in order to be accused, threatened, exposed, emotionally blackmailed or nagged by a lover; after all, you've already got a spouse who may do that. You *must* hold a profound belief that your lover wants only the best for you and that your happiness and fulfilment are important in his or her mind. Only then will you be comfortable in sharing your secrets and trusting them with your life. You'll use your pre-extramarital affair courtship period for this purpose and we'll be discussing it in greater detail in Chapter 11.

2. You must respect them for who they are.

We form opinions about people every day from only small fragments of information because that information is compared against the internal social profiles that we carry around with us. You will not necessarily find a paramour who is of the same socioeconomic group, religious or cultural background or at the same place in his or her career as you are. If those things aren't important to you or if you are generally a tolerant sort, it won't be an issue. But, if those things do matter, you should be aware of it at the outset because it will gnaw on you later after the bloom of excitement has worn off the relationship a bit. This issue goes beyond mere demographics. There is a series of painful scenes between Dustin Hoffman and Anne Bancroft in *The Graduate*, where it is obvious that, although they share a common environment and social milieu, neither party lying in the hotel bed respects or has anything in common with the other. They're just 'doing it' for doing its sake. The affair soon becomes an ugly mess.

Naturally, you would expect that your affair will be different: the two of you will have a lot in common and be able to talk easily and comfortably about a wide range of topics. That's one of the pleasures to be derived from a good affair. So, if you think that your lover is cute but ditzy or look down on him or her for lacking ambition or culture, it will spill out eventually and start to poison the relationship. If you're going to have trouble respecting him or her just for their good qualities and being who they are, you should not only do them the favour of not getting involved, but you need to do some further examination of yourself and your own motives. Better to search your own conscience now than to dissect your affair later; choose a lover with whom you may feel more comfortable. After all, it should not be your lover's job to be able to memorise pi to 50 places or compare and contrast Florentine and Flemish painting during the High Renaissance. Just who do you think *you* are?

3. You must have a strong, mutual attraction.
You are each taking big risks. But for the emotional-physical linkage of the relationship, you could probably find your emotional sustenance in a much less dangerous way. Therefore, it should not be one-sided. Yes, there are a lot of other aspects to a relationship: sharing and caring about each others problems, encouraging each other in your work life and other pursuits and revelling in each other's triumphs. But physical attraction *is* a powerful thing and it deserves a level of respect that should not be underestimated. You will be carried through a lot of planning and last minute disappointments if, in turn, you carry with you the thought of the exquisite joy you will feel when you and your lover finally fall into each others arms. A relationship that is not constructed of the mortar of mutual attraction will collapse amid anger, frustration and recrimination. What could be worse than someone who longs for another and knows that, when it comes to tumbling into bed, their partner could take it or leave it?

If your beliefs about your potential lover meet these three criteria, that's really great! If you're right, the two of you stand a good chance of bringing each other much joy and happiness.

Making the Choice

This may seem an odd ending to the chapter. After all, didn't you just make a choice? Maybe not. It could well be that you aren't certain, given how long you've know your prospective paramour, that all of the criteria have been met. Should you still go on to the next step? Probably so, because the risk is still low and the potential payoff great. Until now, you have only sinned in your heart (what else is new?) and that status will continue for a while. You have much to learn about each other and may find more than a few surprises which reveal a lively interest or talent you never suspected. If, on the other hand, the doubts raised by reviewing at least the first two standards are still doing pirouettes in your mind, put your current flame on the back burner. Be friendly, learn more about the person and see if your opinion changes or is reconfirmed, but start looking elsewhere. As we discussed earlier, there are hundreds, perhaps thousands of people from whom your lover will emerge. You do not need to rush headlong into a doubtful situation. Have patience. Have courage.

Although unlikely, it's possible that you've hit it big and have met more than one person with whom you feel that a liaison is possible. How do you choose between them, *if they both meet all the criteria*? Easy, actually. The one who turns you on the most. Why? Because the other factors shouldn't be quantitative. You either trust and respect a person or you don't. It's not necessary for a person to have the psyche of an astronaut to be a trustworthy and stable lover and, although you may *admire* one more than the other for their charitable acts, athletic ability or social grace and charm, it is of no concern to you, given the scope of your relationship. After all, if you're going into an affair, your heart (and other organs) should at least be doing an extra pitter-pat.

Popping the Question

If it hasn't come up already, it's time to let your potential paramour know your feelings and intentions. You must do it in a way which, just in case you have misread the situation, leaves you both a graceful out. There are probably an infinite number of ways to adequately express the thoughts you wish to convey. Unlike 'Will you marry me?', however, there is no simple sentence asking someone to be your extramarital lover that doesn't come across as more than a little crude. You will need to string sentences, even paragraphs, together.

The following 'speech' is just a means to give you some typical ones. It's been made purposely redundant so that you can perhaps find some elements that you feel most comfortable with. It shouldn't be memorised. Far from it. It's probably said best in a sincere, but halting, manner.

You know, I really enjoy talking with you; just being with you. You really are very nice. So this is a little hard for me to say and, if it makes you a little uncomfortable, please let me know. When we're not together, I've found myself thinking about you a lot. I realise that I am attracted to you and I feel that you seem interested a bit in me, too. If I've misread you, I apologise, so please tell me right now and I'll drop the subject.

Obviously, we'll have to assume here that you've got a response that is encouraging.

If my personal circumstances were different, this would be a lot simpler. I would have a lot more to give. As you may have guessed, my home situation is not ideal; in fact, even though I can handle it, it's been pretty hard. But knowing you and thinking about you has made it a lot easier. I don't know what your circumstances are or what you feel you need right now to bring you more joy and happiness. If I did know, I would do whatever I could to give it to you.

One would hope that, during this little speech, more encouraging words from your lover-to-be would have been forthcoming. If your comments are greeted with silence, you may ask again if they want to drop the subject or just think about it and discuss it the next time you see each other.

I think that we could bring each other a lot of happiness and joy in many different ways. We could become very special to each other as intimate friends. I don't want you to ever feel, however, that you are obligated to me in any way or owe me anything. You won't. Just knowing you and being with you in the here and now will be enough for me. More than enough. Precious. Anyway, I think I've said a lot. You may want to give it some thought yourself. I understand this is pretty serious and you probably have a few questions rolling around in your mind; I know I do. So if you don't want to talk about it right now, I'll understand.

By now, you should *really* know where you stand. If it's gone well, then (yee-hah!) we're on to the next chapter.

CHAPTER 10

No Time to be Romantic:
Rules First, Mush Second

O*h, boy! Wowee! Hang on to that roller coaster 'cause here you go!* That's probably how you feel, but it can't be the way that you act. Not in public, at least. If the two of you are not to destroy the affair even before it's begun, you will have to be careful. It is absolutely critical that care and attention to detail start at the very beginning, so that habits and understandings are well ingrained. They will pay you tremendous dividends in the happier years ahead. You must both begin by setting out the basic ground rules of how you are going to handle your courtship *before* you become lovers.

When you're single, it's understood that you're dating with the purpose of forming a deeper relationship. Meeting for a cup of coffee or a meal, going to a movie or sporting event all carry the cultural message that the future is involved – a public future. When two married people strike up a conversation on a train, at a school function or at a charity fundraiser, there is no cultural imperative. It will be what they choose to make of it and it will be, at its essence, private.

The first rules couples usually have to make involve communications: the places, numbers, number of times and times of day that either can make or receive a call. Also high on the list should be what to do or say if someone else answers the phone. What name or message should be given that will arouse the least suspicion? Is e-mail safe? Should an alias be used? If you use pagers, should you have a secret code to encrypt your messages or identities? What restrictions should be placed on the use of mobile phones for either making or receiving calls? By the way, we'll be discussing mobile phones, pagers and the problems of other modern conveniences later on in Chapter 15. The point is, everyone's circumstances are always a little different, so you have to establish comprehensive rules that you will not only know, *but also abide by.*

The next set of rules usually involves meeting in public places: do you acknowledge each other if you meet while either of you is in the company of someone else? If so, do you make honest introductions or do you have aliases? Do you have a way to signal each other to avoid contact so that your cover can't accidentally be blown by one of you in the presence of the other? Too paranoid? Not really. What could be worse than unexpectedly seeing your lover on the street, running over and throwing your arms around him or her, only to find that your beloved has been at lunch with the boss who had just bent down to tie his shoelace and was out of your field of view? Only one thing – substituting the spouse for the boss.

The third set of rules is one most lovers-to-be don't usually think of: what to do when your lover *doesn't* appear at the appointed place and time. Because it's not solemnised by law, your relationship may tend to feel more fragile than it really is; this will often cause unnecessary worry, almost of the kind one has for a child. Your first reaction may be 'Oh my God, there's been an accident', or that the spouse has got wise and there is a major confrontation going on at that very moment. However, 99.999% of the time, that's just not so. Usually it's something mundane, such as a traffic tie-up, an unexpected phone call or last-minute meeting. Sometimes it may just be a lunch offer that your lover realises better be accepted lest some suspicion be aroused by a change in behaviour. This is where flexibility, stability and maturity in both your lover *and* yourself are paramount. Neither of you should panic or do something adversely affecting the other aspects of your life, solely because you want to capture a few more moments together. Sure, you're disappointed. But, after an agreed-upon period of time, you have to be able to shrug your shoulders and say 'that's life' and fill up the time you would have had with your paramour by doing something else or make alternative arrangements to see that the rest of your day goes as planned. The key point is to agree on a precise amount of time when you should stop waiting for each other; this will not only let the party waiting know not to wait, but will reassure the lover unable to make the assignation that his or her absence is not causing unnecessary anxiety and frustration.

Congratulations! You've completed the next major phase in taking you to a happier, better place. If this section of the book was a fun part, the next will be a true delight. See you there.

SECTION C

Beginning Your Affair

CHAPTER 11

The Pre-extramarital Courtship

Well, you've found your lover, or so you think, and you're already giddy with anticipation. Go back and look at some of the earlier chapters about telling behaviour and the uncertainty of relationships. I know. You're *still* giddy with anticipation, but, so far, no one seems to have picked up on it. Good. But this next part is going to take a lot of control because everything inside you wants to rush it. Don't. Savour it, instead.

If you are lucky, the two of you will soon be stepping off into the abyss of passion. It will be nice if you can make it a round trip. That takes some thought and sharing. It means being emotionally committed to one another before you slide out of your undies. And the way you do that is almost old-fashioned. The two of you are in a situation not unlike young, chaste lovers planning to elope against your parents' wishes.

121

Like Leigh, to whom you were introduced at the beginning of this book, many times you and your lover will already have been good friends before a romantic relationship begins to blossom. For others, there is an instant, almost wild, attraction that can be very intimidating. Yet you have a real dread that it's dangerous to act upon your emotions so quickly. What do you do? Simple things. Normal things. Rather than meet for a sit-down meal, you should bring a packed lunch or pick up some takeaway, and take a walk. But why not chat over lunch? Because, you will be staring too much and too often into each others' eyes, looking for clues to see if your previous comments were acceptable. That's too heavy a burden for both speaker and listener. Better to walk and turn to look into each others' eyes only now and then; it will make those glances that much more special and free you up to choose your words more slowly and carefully and be a better listener, as well. If the weather is nice, go to a park, hold hands, enjoy the experience of nature. If you can find a place to safely steal a kiss, do it, but it's no time for any under the shirt or up the leg groping. It's a foolish risk to make out like a couple of teenagers in public. Be patient and remember that soon there will come a time when each of you will be able to slowly and sweetly luxuriate in the caresses of the other.

If the outdoors is less than appealing, stroll around the shops without window shopping too much. Talk to each other. A lot. What about? You have lots to discuss. But, sooner or later, you'll start getting into the more specific and, if you're getting comfortable with each other, more erotic than embarrassing subjects: your hopes and expectations for your affair; your likes and dislikes in romance: candlelight or darkness? Music or poetry? Champagne or red wine? (If your paramour-to-be says 'crack cocaine', you may have a problem); birth control and protecting each other from sexually transmitted diseases. These last two items belong on your 'must discuss' list *before* you get into bed. 'Bring condoms? I thought you said you were on the pill!'

What does all this conversation do? By the time you are ready to consummate your affair, you will be pretty good friends. When you finally do get into bed, your only agenda will be to please each other and share love. You will not feel embarrassed, defiant or afraid to get naked with each other because you know that this is no battle between the sexes. You are on the same side.

CHAPTER 12

The First Time

Nervous? I'll bet! But you should also be about as excited as a six-year-old on Christmas Eve. This is where all that trustworthiness and maturity is going to be sorely tested. I sure hope you haven't shared your stories of anticipation with anyone other than, your therapist, if you've got one.

More than for any other event in your relationship, this one will take thorough planning. Forget spontaneity. What you should both be striving for is to prepare an environment for yourselves in which you will feel, to the greatest extent possible, secure, comfortable and at ease. After all, preparation is what makes astronauts feel better about a launch of the space shuttle, and they have even more to lose than you do, if something goes wrong.

The most obvious and pressing questions usually centre

around logistics or, as US real-estate magnate William P. Zeckendorf put one aspect of it, 'Location, location, location.' No matter how secure or safe it may seem, don't use the residence of either party. Not only because of the risk that you might be discovered, either directly or by some telltale bit of evidence, but also because other factors will intrude. First, the marital abode is emotionally charged. The marital bed even more so. It will be difficult to relax, be your happiest and perform your best if there are photographs and mementoes of your or your lover's domestic life. Besides, the phone might ring.

Does a friend have a place that has been offered to you for such uses? Think twice. You may trust your friend implicitly, but juicy secrets are hard to keep and romance inspires a variety of emotions in outside observers. You may even come away with the lingering feeling that you have had an invisible third person in bed with you. Besides, again, the phone might ring.

A tryst in a secluded area of a public park is not a safe way to begin. Either because lawbreakers will be around, in which case you will be exposed to *real* danger, or law enforcers will be around, in which case you will be exposed, period.

You'll probably have to acknowledge that the wisest plan of action is to get a hotel room. After all, isn't that what your love nestegg is primarily for? Even in our non-sexist world, this is a job probably best left to the man. (A woman checking around may make the hotel staff wonder if the sex that will be taking place in the room will be of a commercial nature, and that's the only kind of illicit sex they're really concerned about.) Here again, advance planning is the key. You should not be wasting valuable time on the day you consummate your affair in the nerve-wracking and unsexy activity of hunting down a hotel with vacancies. Turn ahead to Chapter 16 'Love in the Proper Venue', for specifics on choosing, reserving and paying for a hotel room consistent with your needs and resources.

The day of your delight arrives. From the moment you get up, you must be focused on the here and now and masking any telling behaviour. Summon all the concentration and calm that you have (this is where the meditation will come in handy). Eat your usual breakfast; wear your usual clothes. For the sake of your lover, do not wear any cologne, perfume, perfumed soap or oil; you should have pretty much cut that out, remember? If only one of you still smokes, the smoker should have recently washed his or her hair and put on freshly laundered clothes. Try to avoid smoking today, if you can. If it's a weekend day and you usually wear your grubbies, wear them today. If you are ostensibly going out to do chores, run errands or partake in some outdoor activity, make sure that your manner of dress and your accessories are appropriate. If you usually shower later in the day, rather than earlier, don't shower (hotels do have those things, you know). Hard as it may be, don't rush to get out of the house any more than usual.

Have you planned how you are going to account for your time today? If you're supposed to be running errands that does not involve buying anything that could spoil without refrigeration (if not in the dead of winter), then you may have been able to take care of some of the items the previous day and store them in a place your spouse hadn't noticed in the past twelve hours. You may also want to be sure that you have a comb or brush in the car. It should have been in there weeks ago because we didn't want telling behaviour, right? (And remember, it will *only* be for your use.) The more numerous and diversely located the errands you have to do, the better. You should have paid for those items by cheque, rather than credit card and dated the cheque ahead to today. Make sure that those items are back in your car *before* you leave the house (perishables you can buy on the way home).

I know you want today to be special. It will be. And without bringing the usual accoutrements of romance. Forget flowers, cards, alcohol, chocolate or gifts of any kind. Those you can do later in your relationship. Right now, they will only be another detail that you will have to keep track of and cover up. A single fallen rose petal on a car's passenger side carpet will raise a load of hassle. Neither of you need the extra anxiety. And, after all, you are giving *yourself*. For your lover, that will be a thousand times more meaningful than a bouquet.

Do you and your waiting-to-be lover have all of your signals straight? You should not have to make *any* telephone contact. If one of you is late or can't show up, the other knows what to do and not to worry. Have patience and try not to be too disappointed. If you are right in your assessment of your beloved, there *will* be another day. If you are wrong, be grateful that there isn't.

You should both know the hotel or motel's location and layout beforehand. If you're both driving, take separate cars and park on different sides of the motel in such a place as to allow the party getting the room key to be able to signal the other from a side entrance or open any locked door. It's probably best to go up to the room separately, about five or ten minutes apart, depending on whether either one of you needs to shower or feels a bit shy.

I won't tell you what to do now, except to take your time, be reassuring and relax. Don't go for simultaneous orgasms, exotic sexual positions or the like. You don't need to prove what a masterful love technician you are; only that you are grateful, appreciative, considerate and generous. Knocking each other's socks off can come later. It shouldn't even surprise you if one or both of you are too nervous to perform; don't feel inadequate or disappointed. *It doesn't matter; there will be other days.* For this time, at least, just talk to each other, laugh and enjoy.

After you've rearranged yourselves and said your sweet, happy-sad good-byes, don't head straight home, even if you will be later than expected. You will need a little time to decompress and get back into 'normal world' mode. Run your last few errands. And wipe that smile off your face!

CHAPTER 13

Managing the Delirium Factor

I*t's two o'clock in the morning and your spouse is fast asleep. You, on the other hand, have just woken up. Your heart is pounding and you have the following eloquent question and answer rolling over again and again inside your head: 'Did I really do that? Holy shit! I really did it!' After saying that to yourself a few times, you will try to carefully recall every detail of the day, over and over.*

It's OK. Allow yourself about an hour of this fun and then try to get some sleep. It's even all right to hug your spouse if that helps you calm down; besides, it's a good reality check.

The day after is going to be a lot tougher. Mentally replaying the previous day will give way to making lists of questions: is your lover OK? Did they get away with it as well as you did? Are they still looking forward to seeing you again? Did they really enjoy your time together as much as you did? Do the two of you think you're in love? You are *dying* to make that phone call or see your beloved again immediately. It's going to be really, really hard, but *stick to your prearranged rules. Always.* Watch yourself for telling behaviour; be vigilant. Listen to yourself, too: are you whistling or humming a tune? Is it more loud or upbeat than your usual vocalisings? It certainly better not be 'My No-Tell Lover', 'One Night Love Affair', 'Saving All My Love For You', or any one of dozens of other pop songs that might be a fitting reference to your circumstances. If you're going to be around the house all day with your spouse in some proximity, don't dote on him or her to overcompensate; just find something normal to do and really do it.

Another odd reaction to these events can come over you: you may feel a strong urge to blow your cover! Two different psychological forces are at play, but they can reinforce each other to the great detriment of your affair, your lover and yourself: first, when we have good news or a great secret, we just naturally want to share our good fortune to see the delight in the face of others mirroring and validating our own. Secondly, you may feel guilty for being so happy 'at the expense' of your spouse who has now been 'wronged'. You relieve your guilt by robbing yourself of the opportunity for future enjoyment and by bringing down the wrath of the multitudes upon yourself. Many psychologists who deal with these issues every day have come to the conclusion that it is not the affair that ruins a marriage, but the emotional turmoil that results when the participating spouse's activities are revealed to the other. No good will come to anyone from taking that step. Don't do it.

It's also during this time that you may feel that you must talk to someone, other than your lover, about your affair or you will positively burst. If you've simply got to do it in order to avoid more telling behaviour, choose that person carefully. Not by 'how good a friend' they are, but based on your assessment of their ability to keep a secret, any secret, in general. If you have one of them as a friend, confide in a person who keeps secrets as an integral part of his or her profession: a therapist, doctor, lawyer, accountant, tax adviser, etc., and *say* that you would expect them to keep this in confidence as they would any information they acquired in their professional setting. The chances that they'll let something slip are at least less likely.

Despite your best efforts, there will be at least some change in you; that's OK, it's inevitable, which is why you began altering your behaviour months ago. The little extra lilt in your voice and bounce in your step is just another iteration. But do be careful; as we noted above, success breeds success, but it can also produce arrogance and sloppiness as offspring. And, as we all know, guys and gals, pride goeth before a fall.

SECTION D

Managing Stealth:
Keeping Your Affair Private
in an Unprivate World

CHAPTER 14

The Scope of the Problem:
Your Fingerprints are Everywhere

From the moment that you and your paramour become lovers, you will need to devote a significant amount of attention to keeping your secret love secret. After all, within the close circles of your lives, it is the hottest, juiciest news of the year. And you don't have to be pursued by the paparazzi to know that individual privacy ain't what it used to be. With each modern convenience which high technology offers and we embrace, we unthinkingly barter away a piece of our lives.

It is a Monday morning in mid-autumn, 1984. The Dutch electronics manufacturer Philips has recently introduced a new product, the compact disc player; it provides great sound, but is very expensive and there are only a handful of titles available for purchase. The top-of-the-line desktop computer is the IBM PC-AT which has a 15-megabyte hard drive in place of one of its 5-1/4" floppy drives. A new company, Compaq, is now selling a portable computer about the size and weight of a fully stuffed piece of carry-on luggage.

At the offices of one of the fledgling mobile telephone companies, the president is holding his weekly cabinet meeting. The Chief Financial Officer has just reviewed the September financials. He notes that, even though new customer sales have been increasing at a blinding pace, the average revenue per customer has been dropping for the past three months in a row; not only are new customers using the phone less than old customers, but the old customers are using the phone less, as well. Unless the stream of revenue from the existing customer base can be increased, the company will not reach its target for the year.

The company's vice president of marketing has been prepared for this and starts in on her solution: among the company's offerings that has so far been a dud is itemised billing, the ability to receive a printout on your monthly statement of every mobile, just like with your land-line. Although every customer is told about the service in their introductory package, and descriptive inserts have been put in monthly bills, only a few customers, mostly lawyers who want to be able to bill clients for their time while driving, have signed up for the service. Despite being priced fairly cheaply, it's got a high profit margin because the only incremental costs to the company are the postage and extra paper to print the bill; the company's digital telephone switch was designed to automatically track the data just as it came from the factory.

She proposes that the company give the service away for a couple of months and see if customers like it enough to continue using the service. Even if only 10% sign up, it will be enough to get the company's revenues back on track.

'I've got a problem, Chief,' says the general counsel, a pudgy lawyer in his fifties and almost a decade older than everyone else in the room. There is a chorus of good-natured groans from his fellow officers.

'C'mon,' says the Marketing VP, 'we're giving the thing away, for God's sake, and we were told that no change in our tariffs was required. What could be illegal about this?'

'It's not illegal. I just think its a mistake from the customer-relations standpoint, because we may catch more flak from this than we gain in revenues and may even end up losing customers. I'll bet that a lot of these guys use their car phones to call their girlfriends because it's the only time they can talk when there's no one else around. If the bill goes to the house and the wife opens it up, she's going to want to know what number was called twenty times that month. His cover's going to be blown and he will not be a happy camper.'

After the hoots and catcalls have subsided, the president reluctantly chooses to take the gamble and go ahead with the itemised billing promotion. Six weeks later, all hell breaks loose.

How far we have come since then in the lowering of our expectations of privacy! We all know now that, whether we are at home or at work, all of our local calls are being tracked and stored and that they can be recalled and documented upon demand. Thanks to Caller ID, no one with an unlisted number expects that they can make a phone call and maintain the integrity of that privacy without going through an extra step and alerting the recipient that they are blocking their outgoing number. Make one purchase at a specialty store and, unless you pay by cash and refuse to give your e-mail or telephone number to the sales assistant, your letterbox will soon be barraged with junk. (I bought my nephew a fishing rod for Christmas three years ago over the telephone and I've been getting bow hunting catalogues ever since.) If you use a credit or debit card, not only are your spending and cashing habits recorded, but also a mosaic of your whereabouts through time is constantly being created and updated.

Every time you use your computer to visit an Internet site or send or receive a piece of e-mail, you create another entry into a database about yourself that can be accessed by thousands of groups and individuals unknown to you. At the same time, others – your employer, doctor, insurance company, etc. – are creating and sharing databases about you, as well. Even your genetic code, the unique arrangement of your DNA that makes you you, is not protected from prying eyes.

So far, all we have been talking about is data that is being created 'passively', i.e. in the ordinary course of business and everyday events. What happens when someone takes a particular interest in you?

Former Colorado Senator Gary Hart was a leading candidate for the Democratic nomination for US president when rumours surfaced that he was having an affair. In addition to issuing the usual denials, *he challenged the press to find evidence.* What an idiot!!! It took them less than a week. Naturally, in no time at all, his campaign had self-destructed and his 'secret love' had taken off her clothes for 3 million *Playboy* readers (more than half of whom probably said to themselves, 'Now I see why he did it.').

You may have seen Gene Hackman appear in a great movie called *The Conversation*. It's about a private investigator using state-of-the-art audio equipment to track an adulterous and maybe murderous couple. If you haven't, I recommend it. Since then, the technology of snooping, like the technology of everything else in the past few decades, has jumped by light-years to the point where equipment can be purchased at bargain-basement prices which will exceed anything the CIA had available when the movie was made. Is your spouse suspicious enough to act on his or her concerns? Unless you and your lover adopt the lifestyle of the Unabomber, someone bent on tracking you down and exposing your affair will manage to do so. A modern private investigator will probably be able to do it in a few days at most. And they will start by logging on to their computer. Indeed, the computer has become the primary means by which we purposely gather information and unintentionally give away information about ourselves.

Your spouse won't need to hire a private investigator to do a pretty credible snoop job of his or her own. One of several personal research programs currently available is 'Net Detective', which bills itself as 'The Easy Way to Find Out Anything About Anyone', and includes a testimonial from a woman who brags about learning the amount of her neighbour's credit problems, alimony and child support. In the summer of

2000, that computer program was selling in the US for a mere $25.00. Another kind of program, screen recording software such as BBF Flashback, records PC and Internet activity much like a camcorder, taking a 'snapshot' of the screen (every second, if desired) that can be played back later.

Of course, for every intelligence-gathering technique, there's counterintelligence, and one such product, OnTrack's Internet Cleanup software, is designed to wipe cookies, files and other unused cache artifacts out of the user's hard drive. Another one, the SurfSecret Deluxe, can be run in 'Stealth Mode', making it invisible to local PC and network administrators, and automatically wipes out selected files and folders.

Counterintelligence or no, the moral is obvious. Lest it be missed, however, I have emphasised it here: *the only way you will be able to prevent your affair from being ultimately discovered is to prevent it from being seriously suspected.*

You will notice that there are two key modifiers here: 'ultimately' and 'seriously'. They are there for a reason. 'Ultimately' means that you do have *some* time in which to get things settled down. 'Seriously' means that your spouse has to be moved to taking the kind of steps that most decent people would categorise as 'being a first-class snoop', i.e., they have to be ready to undertake the kind of behaviour that, if itself is discovered, would seriously undermine the marriage. What follows in the next chapter, then, is what many of you, no matter what the status of your relationships, will probably want most to know.

CHAPTER 15

The Way of *Yoda*:
Control and Management of the Details
of Everyday Life

Yoda, the *Star Wars* character who serves as Luke Skywalker's Zen Buddhist Merlin, teaches his protégé that, in order to get in touch with what is best and most powerful within himself, he must learn to master and remove the distractions that take up his life. These distractions are not removed simply by forgetting about them or paying them no heed; they are removed by making what now requires conscious thought and effort something which is automatic, thus freeing the thinking self for greater things.

We do a lot of this ourselves already through the habits we have learned over the course of our lives. Those habits remove the decision-making process and distractions that would otherwise keep us from the rest of our day's tasks. We don't need a checklist to be certain that we have washed all of the critical areas when we shower or that we have put our socks on before our shoes. We don't have to remember the steps of penmanship or the location of the letters on a keyboard when we write someone a note.

The exercises in Chapter 8 served a dual purpose: not only were you supposed to learn something about yourself, but also you were beginning to develop habits that would make the conduct of your future affair less burdensome and, therefore, more enjoyable. When a behaviour becomes a habit, there is no 'tell,' because no signal is being sent out with it.

The first part of your job, then, is to learn what behaviour, when attached to a 'tell', is recognisable and becomes capable of arousing suspicion over time. Or, to put it more bluntly, how did others in your circumstances get tripped up and set off the suspicions in their spouses that led to their affair's discovery?

Just like building a criminal case, the investigator-prosecutor-jury (your spouse) relies on eyewitness testimony, direct or physical evidence, circumstantial evidence and expert-witness testimony. Like the law enforcer, the spouse's work involves bringing together various threads to determine whether there is sufficient evidence to convict you. Let's look at each of these in greater detail to see what happened.

Direct Testimony

Someone you know sees the two of you together. It happens more often than you might expect, even in a big city where you think you're anonymous. You are never truly anonymous. Remember the 'Six Degrees of Separation' mentioned earlier? When the subject of the connectedness of all of us was brought up previously, it was to let you know that there were many people who you had the chance of meeting. It works the other way, too, but it takes only two degrees: someone who knows you and also knows someone else you know.

The Chicago metropolitan area has a population exceeding 7 million. Judy K. lives in a wealthy suburb twenty miles north of the Loop. She arranged to meet her lover in the middle of the week in a singles bar-restaurant in a solidly middle-class suburb 35 miles southwest from her home. In a high-rise office building, two miles from the restaurant, a fellow who was her next-door neighbour ten years before now works as an executive in a start-up business. He's also moved to a different neighbourhood, about three miles from Judy's, so he sees her husband from time to time at the local health club. One Wednesday evening a month, the company staff goes to that same bar to let off steam and kick around ideas in an informal setting. Judy and her lover are playing kissy-face in a booth. Suddenly she locks eyes with her ex-neighbour carrying a couple of pitchers of beer and turns bright red. He mouths the words 'No problem', turns and walks back to his fellow workers. She has no choice but to believe him and vows to herself that that is the last time she'll ever go out in public with her lover again.

We all like a little excitement, but, I guarantee you, nothing can kill a romantic evening more than this kind of close call.

Direct or Physical Evidence

When a spouse thinks that they've 'got the goods', this is what they're usually talking about. We've already discussed the cyber-swamp of computers, so let's look at the other everyday objects which can provide the evidence that can serve to entrap, especially in our high-tech world. We'll start with the simpler electronic devices that can cause big problems.

1. Telephones: Stored Number and Redial Features

These are really useful conveniences when you are in a hurry. What they have in common are an electronic memory and the ability to dial accurately faster than most humans are capable of. The problem, of course, is, while they have a perfect memory, they have no discretion and will yield up their information readily.

> *Charlie D., married fourteen years: Last year, I noticed that we had been getting more wrong-number calls than previously. It seemed to happen a lot just as I was heading out the door to my cycling club's Saturday-morning run. One day, I forgot my wallet and had to come back into the house to get it. Laurie got off the phone really quick when I came into the bedroom. I stopped to pick up the phone to tell one of my friends that I was running late and accidentally hit the redial button. A man answered immediately and said, 'Hi, hon, is everything OK?'*

Obviously, it wasn't.

2. Caller ID

Telephone exchanges use its precursor, Automatic Number Identification, when communicating with each other for billing purposes. From the day this feature became available, it was controversial. It is essentially an electronic device which picks up the calling number transmitted to it by the local telephone exchange and displays it on a LCD screen. The device may either be in a separate box which connects between the wall outlet and the telephone instrument, or is part of the telephone itself. On the positive side, the customer can tell if anyone is making threatening, harassing or prank phone calls (provided that they don't block their number, as we'll mention later) and can have the option in advance to either answer or ignore a call from annoying or deadbeat friends or relatives. On the other hand, there were legitimate needs for privacy: what if a battered spouse who had taken shelter from her abusive husband in a friend's home wanted to talk to her teenage kids still living with their father? If he looked at the phone, he could find out where she was, endangering her safety. What if you wanted to call a bank's hotline to find out what the current mortgage interest rate was? The bank would automatically have your name on a list for refinancing and salespeople to call on you without your permission. When push came to shove, a compromise was reached: numbers would be automatically sent unless the caller took an extra step to block their outgoing call.

Lilian F.: This didn't happen to me but a friend of mine suspected something was going on with her husband; they had bought a new phone and each programmed five numbers into it; some of her husband's numbers were women whom she didn't know. She called up the phone company and ordered Caller ID and then went out to

Radio Shack and bought a Caller ID box and hid it under the dresser. She and her husband work different shifts and she reviewed the incoming numbers every day for about a week; the same number kept coming up about the same time every day. Well, one day he had to work a different shift. When the call came in, she told the woman that she was his sister and knew about the affair. By the time his 'sister' was through chatting with his girlfriend, she knew EVERYTHING.

The husband's missteps in this case went far beyond mere issues of technology, and we'll be discussing those later on.

3. Mobile Phones

Earlier we described the mobile phone itemised billing detail promotion from the naïve perspective of the service provider. Here's how Brian B., one of their customers, recalls his perspective on the Marketing VP's proposal:

I thought that a mobile phone might allow me to spend Saturday afternoons in hotels with my girlfriend while I was 'at work'. It worked great until the first bill came; I didn't know that called numbers would be listed and never guessed that my wife would open it before I did. She called every number on the bill she didn't recognise, including my girlfriend's home and pager and even the hotel where we stayed. The clerk even confirmed my name, address and check-in date.

Not surprisingly, Brian didn't feel like describing what happened next.

4. Pagers

Like telephones and other electronic devices, pagers have come a long way. In the beginning, persons who wanted to reach the customer had to call a special number belonging to the paging company and leave a message; the company would then send out a signal to the pager, which merely emitted a single tone alerting the customer to call the paging company and hear the message from an operator-clerk. It's range was limited to a radius of a few dozen miles and, just like the telephones of yore, all pagers were black. Within little more than a decade, pagers came to rival mobile telephones in versatility and convenience for the price, having alpha-numeric displays, privacy codes, date and time of call records, caller ID, vibrating or beeping alert, national or international reach and a variety of designs and colours.

Denise M., married 21 years, now separated: My husband, Phil, has had a beeper for almost as long as I can remember. Each time he got a new one with more features and a new number, he'd have to teach me the routine of how it worked if I wanted to reach him. One day he brought home a new one and I offered to read the instruction manual and save him the time of going through it with me. Over the next few months I began to notice when different features were used, like the 'locking' position that cleared off the other pages and only showed a selected one or when it was set on beep or vibrate. I knew he always had it with him, but he'd sometimes say that he didn't get my page. Well, I started up a new business after the kids went away to school and I thought I needed a pager myself. His paging company was offering a special on second pagers so I signed up. One morning, Phil was rushing to get to work and took my pager instead. Since I couldn't reach him directly, I thought that every time he got a page, I'd just send the identical message to my pager, then we'd just switch back when he got home. I got some pretty racy messages; it took everything I had, but I forwarded them to him. I told him what I'd done when he came in the door and then I just let him have it.

5. Credit Cards

Although we probably don't think of them as electronic devices, that's exactly what our credit cards are. The sales assistant plugs them into the international database just as surely as we log on to the Internet with our home PCs. Some people in the midst of an affair will actually charge the bill at a *local hotel* on a credit card whose statement is sent to the home, or use that same card to purchase merchandise at the most expensive jeweller in town or the local Janet Reger outlet. I can only surmise that they somehow *want* to get caught so that they can have the confrontation with their spouse that they've been avoiding but realise is necessary. Far more often, however, it is the less dramatic purchases that raise suspicions: petrol purchased across town, rather than at the neighbourhood station or a lunch purchased at a local restaurant when you were ostensibly on the road.

It doesn't take high technology to create suspicions in a spouse. There can be telling artifacts that are less obvious than those listed in the Carly Simon song discussed in Chapter 8.

Here are a few that are among the most commonly mentioned:

1. Receipts, brochures or maps associated with out-of the-ordinary purchases or places.
2. Matchbooks from resorts, nightclubs or expensive restaurants never mentioned to spouse.
3. Flower petals or pieces of gift wrap in car or clothes.
4. A hairbrush or other 'artifacts' in the car not appropriate to the sex of the driver.
5. New smells or unidentified hairs on clothing.
6. Unaccounted-for withdrawals of large sums of money.
7. Herpes or other sexually transmitted disease!! (More on that later.)

We don't need to even mention love letters, greeting cards, photographs, engraved mementos and other objects that are about as damning as being caught *in flagrante*.

Circumstantial Evidence

With this kind of evidence, there's no direct linkage to any activity in the outside world or the spousal relationship; rather it's an 'innocent' activity that is out of the ordinary.

For both sexes:

1. Breath 'condiments', i.e. the use of gum or mints as a new habit.
2. New, differently styled and/or more colourful underwear.
3. Increasing amounts of exercise and/or weight loss.
4. Change to less conservative dress and/or hair style, growing hair longer.
5. Interest in new hobbies or sports.

6. New keys on keychain.

7. Boxers, briefs, panties or tights on inside out when coming home at night.

For men:

1. Clothes missing.

2. Shaving beard and dressing better on the weekends.

3. Hair combed differently from when having left home.

For women:

1. Increase in frequency of painting finger and toenails.

2. New (imaginary) female friend.

3. Spending significantly more time on the telephone talking with female friends; inaudible conversation punctuated by laughter.

4. Keeping pubic hair neatly trimmed.

Expert Testimony (Your Spouse's)

You have been living with your spouse probably for many years, maybe decades. You therefore also are likely to have a pretty good sense of what constitutes typical behaviour towards you and those around you. Whether you call it carrying a 'personality profile' on your spouse, observation or intuition, you can almost 'feel' when something isn't quite right. Although it's the least quantifiable, it is probably the most common way in which an affair is suspected. At the risk of being sexist, this sixth sense seems to be far better developed in women than men. It is to be respected.

At a recent gathering of women who wanted to share their recollections of discovering their present or former husbands' affairs, their experiences were almost uniform:

Kelley G.: *He began getting home late from work and being more distant; he suddenly seemed to spend more time with his 'friends' and became evasive or defensive when I asked him questions. He often seemed preoccupied and was less affectionate.*

Marilyn J.: *That was Bob, all right. Shifty eyes, shifty body, defensive on everything. His favourite was to turn the conversation around so that I ended up being the bad guy.*

Karen P.: *Looking back on it gives you a different perspective. Now I see that Rick picked arguments with me as an excuse to leave the house to get a chance to be with his lover. He used to call me several times during the day. It was always a short call about some little thing; now I see that it was probably to pinpoint my location and reduce his chances of getting caught (we live in a pretty small town). His schedule seemed to change too so that he couldn't make any commitments and, of course, the amount of 'quality time' we had together went down big time.*

Rose M.: *I am a survivor of an affair of my husband three years ago. It was the change in routine that first made me notice; not showing up after work at the usual time with no particular excuse as to why. A little later it was verbal abuse and letting you know that nothing you do seems to make him happy. During the day-to-day interaction and at night, too, he seemed to 'shut off' and be remote.*

Danielle T.: *Well, I guess this means that I got 'the Usual', too. No physical stuff — sex, touching, cuddling, - and the emotional games — loves you one day, moody and withdrawn the next. It made me start looking for stuff which now seems pretty obvious: hotel charges that didn't correspond to his business trips, unexpected extension of a trip, overnight flight delays, and those prepaid phone cards; why would he need them when we have both home and business telephone credit cards we use every day practically? It took me almost six months to figure it out. Now I don't know which one of us was dumber. If you have enough unexplained and unreasonable information to even suspect that your mate is cheating on you, there's a 95% chance that he is.*

If this chapter has done nothing else, it should make it abundantly clear how much maturity, discipline and planning is required to maintain your clandestine affair. Success will depend on following certain rules requiring self-awareness, self-control, planning and sensitivity to your spouse's moods and perceptions. These rules should, of course, apply to both you *and* your lover. These attributes will do more than help maintain stealth; they will provide dividends to your life and those around you which we will discuss in later chapters.

1. *Be aware of and maintain the current level of physical intimacy with your spouse.*

If you have any kind of sex life with your spouse at all, never, *ever* let it get worse or go bad. Listen to your spouse's complaints and wishes and, if you can, do your best to act on them immediately. Waiting a few weeks may make it seem like you're bringing home a technique from your lover; there's nothing more unnerving than introducing a little trick to your spouse and hearing 'Where did you learn *that*?'

2. Make all of the changes to your life described in the previous chapters as slowly as you can stand.

Of course you are anxious to get on with it. But this is where developing control and habits will pay the biggest dividends. If losing weight is part of your plan, do it gradually. Although it is tempting to get lots of new clothes similar to ones that you've bought recently, don't make redundant purchases; try replacing the most worn-out parts of your wardrobe with smaller sizes first. Don't ask your spouse to comment on your appearance and, if they do notice that you've lost weight, if you think you're capable of it, feign mild surprise at their observation and scepticism as to its validity. If you plan to take up a new activity as a screen, try to get your spouse to be the one to reject participation in it with you.

3. Do your best to be psychologically 'appropriate'.

This is a key part of knowing yourself and your reactions. Don't be withdrawn, sullen or moodier than usual; don't pick fights. Conversely, don't be so cheery and helpful as to border on the weird.

4. Create no record trail.

It is better to lose money on an attempted refund, because you lack a receipt, than to keep copies of transaction slips. Delete all e-mail, no matter how much fun it is to reread because it is so sweet, loving, cute, precious, etc. Learn how to dump your computer cache so that there are no telltales on your hard drive. For necessary paper transactions, i.e. love nestegg bank account records, get a post office box.

5. Keep your electronic features and gizmos to a minimum, encrypt your communications and be certain that you and your lover scrupulously follow the ground rules for contact that you have agreed upon.

At least the options that are tacked on when you buy a car you can use or aesthetically appreciate. But when was the last time you used three-way calling or no-answer-busy-transfer? Speed dialling is a nice convenience, but storing your lover's number is an invitation to disaster at the slip of a finger. It should be obvious by now that you can and should live without itemised billing. Do you really believe that call waiting's benefits outweigh its annoyances and disadvantages?

What if you must have certain telecommunications devices and functionalities?

Home telephone: Ideally, you should never call your lover from home because, even though it's not on your bill, a record has been created which can be recalled upon customer request for up to several months after the call occurs, depending on the company you subscribe to. If you do make a call to either your lover or some other number related to your relationship and you have automatic redial on your home phone, you should get into the habit of clearing out *every* number *every* time you call. Just depress the receiver, lift and hit one or two numbers; that'll do it. Your lover should never call you from home either, especially if you have caller ID. You and your lover may BOTH want to have your numbers blocked by the phone company on an outgoing basis so that they won't show up on the other end, especially if you forget to dial the outgoing call block code. And remember, if you fail to clear your redial, your spouse may be curious as to why you were blocking your number, since the code will show up on the display!

Vehicle-installed mobile phones: Here again, don't order itemised billing detail and don't store numbers you don't want to share. Redial is a very useful feature in a car phone and I won't counsel you not to use it; just get into the habit of pressing 'clr' *every* time you leave the car, whether you've used the phone to call your lover or not. Mobile time is still expensive, despite the ads and promotions. If you get into the habit of talking with your lover often on the phone, two things will happen: first, you will have more busy signals if your spouse tries to call you, which raises suspicions, and, second, your phone bill will also rise sharply, again raising red flags. As long as we're at it, don't even *think* about having call waiting or, if you absolutely must have it for business reasons, of answering call waiting while you and your lover are on the line; it could well be your spouse. Switching back and forth between your spouse and your lover on your tiny handset is not just nerve-wracking; it's an open invitation for disaster because tells will spill out all over the place and a slip-up of some kind is almost inevitable.

Finally, remember that the tighter your budget becomes from paying for all of those minutes, the more difficult it will be to save for your love nestegg.

If you have a mobile, try to break yourself of the habit of carrying it with you everywhere. It's the one area where you can slowly become absent-minded. Whether or not you leave it at home, if your mobile phone rings, your beloved should be the one person who you know *won't* be on the other end of the line.

Remember that, as we discussed back in Chapter 12, it is better for you and your lover not to have any electronic contact *at all* on the day of your rendezvous and let your 'rules for meeting' govern your plans.

Pagers: This may be one of the best ways to communicate, because you can easily encrypt messages by adopting a simple, prediscussed, shorthand code. One or two numbers can be punched in to say 'Can't make it today', 'I will be latex minutes', 'Thinking of you', etc. Telephone numbers can be scrambled according to an agreed-upon method. Nevertheless, you should try to keep messages sent at 'unsafe' times to an absolute minimum and always clear messages out at the first opportunity.

All of this planning may seem as if it would make your affair less romantic, as if there is some universal law of physics that spontaneity equals romance. Hardly. There is also great romance in the 'conspiracy of lovers', and there, my friend, you are.

You have come through the sweet anxiety and exaltation of consummating your affair. You have used your best efforts and taken all possible steps to preserve its secrecy. You've learned the way of Yoda; may the force be with you!

Now, in order to be able to explore the joys of your affair in an environment as free from anxiety as possible, you will need the co-operation of others – specifically, the hotel industry! Let's discuss that next.

CHAPTER 16

Love in the Proper Venue

For the reasons we discussed in Chapter 12 earlier, the first assignation between you and your lover should ideally occur in a hotel or motel room. This is not a bad idea just because it isn't terribly novel. What about *after* you and your friend have become lovers? Statistically, a majority of affairs occur in the home of one of the affair partners. This is not surprising. But, while this may be economical, the preceding chapters provide ample reason why this is unwise on many levels. Over time, direct discovery by a spouse, a child, a friend, houseworker or other visitor becomes ever more likely, and the opportunities for stray clues to be left behind proliferate. If an affair's revelation is to be avoided, it must be consummated elsewhere. And that 'elsewhere' is usually either at a friend's house or at a hotel. There are a great number of variables to consider when using a friend's place, and you, alone, are the best judge of the long-term sense of such an arrangement, based upon your friend's emotional stability, character and many of those other aspects by which you might even have judged your lover. But we can discuss the hotel option in some detail and the various factors worthy of consideration.

It may seem odd to devote much space to the discussion of hotel-room reservations; after all, you've done it dozens of times: you call the number, give them your name and credit card information and either arrive or cancel before 6.00 p.m. As long as you're quiet and obviously not running a callgirl ring, the hotel management couldn't care less whether the coupling that might be taking place in Room 301 is between two people lawfully married to each other. The days of the sexually snooping house detective are long gone.

There's another obvious reason why hotels won't be terribly hostile to your affair – money. An empty room costs almost as much to maintain as an occupied one and the standard measure of a hotel's success is its occupancy rate; it's how management is judged. Hotels, like jewellery stores, rely on affairs in estimating their revenues and optimal capital investment rates. In short, extramarital lovers are contributors to our national economy. However, having just finished reading the previous chapter, you know that you cannot make this transaction in your business-as-usual manner simply because it creates the kind of paper trail that you will need to avoid. So, read on.

Your review of hotels and motels should begin well before you have started an affair, so that you do not have to waste time later and create awkward moments doing research while your lover waits. Your preparatory work, then, is to methodically scope out and survey the hotels and motels in your area for their price, privacy, policies and ambiance. Let's review each of these separately.

1. Price

As you know, hotels come in all price ranges, depending on location, facilities and level of luxury in the accommodation. Much of what you pay for in the room rate of a high-end hotel you will have no need for: a fancy lobby, convention and meeting room facilities, etc. Depending on your circumstances, however, they *can* have their advantages.

(a) If you and your lover are best able to meet in the greater anonymity of a large city's downtown area, a high-end hotel will provide legitimacy, if you see someone you know. After all, you're probably there for a meeting or business lunch. On the downside, you may be trapped into a conversation from which it may be difficult or awkward to extricate yourself.

(b) Your cars may not be needed and, if they are, they can be parked in any number of places that will not provide the impression to someone who knows your vehicle that you are there for an illicit purpose.

(c) Although high-end hotels are more expensive, they are also more likely to have Day Rates (see *3. policies*, below).

(d) Although you shouldn't go up to the room at the same time, you don't have to enter the hotel separately and signal each other; just act as if you are strangers.

If you don't have the specialised needs just described, first-class hotels really make no sense; not only are they a waste of money, but they also may have more stringent security deposit and credit card policies than less upmarket places.

Price, however, comes at a, well, price. Beyond ambiance, there's the issue of personal safety. A *really* cheap hotel in a remote area raises questions of security for yourself and your lover; nothing is as unsexy as trying to make love while being in mortal fear of robbery, assault, rape and other assorted mayhem. Furthermore, even if you survive such an attack, your affair will probably appear on page 1 of the local paper along with a file photo of the local hospital's A&E entrance. As with everything else, use common sense and strike a balance in your decision-making process.

2. Privacy

Unless you live in an extremely rural area, there are probably several hotels within a ten-mile radius of your home or office. (If you're near a motorway, you might want to expand the radius to twenty miles.) There are probably a number of them that you've never seen. They are, therefore, the best ones to check out first. Using your yellow pages directory and a street map you will be able to locate those places which are out of the way from where either you or your lover live, work or have friends or relatives. Is there an unobtrusive place where you and your lover can park your cars or are all spots right on the road? Are there multiple entrances or only one? As you imagine meeting your lover there, go through the logistics in your mind and see if you are confident that all should go smoothly.

It may be that, due to time constraints, the need to keep large mileage changes hidden, lack of availability of transportation and the like, a long drive to your rendezvous may not be wise. There are alternatives. Thanks to the explosion in business travel, there are now numerous hotels tucked in behind office buildings and shopping centres where you could easily park without arousing suspicion and walk the short distance to the hotel's entrance. There are, of course, some disadvantages: a greater likelihood of seeing someone you know and the higher room rates that such a convenient location can often command. Here again, it's important to look places over thoroughly and assess how comfortable you would be operating in a clandestine mode *before* your begin an affair.

3. Policies

If hotels don't care who's sleeping with whom, what policies do you need to know about? As it turns out, quite a few. One thing you will be interested in is whether the hotel offers 'day rates', lower charges for rooms which are vacated by 5.00 p.m. or some other time specified by management. Using day rates can usually save you almost half the cost of a room.

What problems can arise when paying in cash? Obviously, you're willing to pay in advance (once your lover has also arrived), but that sometimes isn't enough. Giving a credit card provides the hotel with an automatic security deposit, not only if you leave without going to the front desk to pay, but in case you damage the room. Yeah, I know: you and your lover are not the road crew from the Guns 'n' Roses tour that blew into town at 1.30 a.m., coked up and ready to party it down. But you have to remember that, even though they have insurance, it's *their* property you're on. If they insist on an imprint of a card, and you have no alternative places available, find out if they are willing to inspect the room as you leave and then give you the imprint and its copies to tear up. Be sure that they do not call in a charge to your VISA or MasterCard and then call in a credit, because both will then appear on your statement. Clarify this in advance. Hotel staff were not born yesterday.

Some hotel rooms positively reek with the smell of stale tobacco. Fortunately, 'No Smoking' rooms are now commonly available in most places. Unless both of you smoke, you're not going to want telltale odours on your hair or clothing.

Finally, you'll want to know if the hotel has any restrictions on bringing or ordering in food to the room. After a nice romp, it can be a lot of fun, as well as romantic, to share some Chinese food or a pizza in bed with your lover!

4. Ambiance

This, of course, is a matter more of personal preference than anything else. Wasn't there once an advertising slogan used in the US by Holiday Inn: 'The best surprise is no surprise'? Or, to paraphrase Gertrude Stein: 'A Travelodge is a Travelodge is a Travelodge.' But predictability is the big advantage only when you don't have the opportunity to check a place out, and, remember, part of your payment is being used to support nationwide advertising and reservation services and to pony up a portion of the owner's franchise fee. Personally, I've found family-owned non-chain hotels to be a better value and to be more interestingly (sometimes in staggeringly poor taste) decorated. It's sort of a little amusement factor you can share with your lover.[12] After you've been to a variety of hotels, you'll

12 Bed and Breakfasts probably provide the best ambience for the money, but the owners almost invariably live there and are more concerned about what goes on under their roofs; they're noisier, too, by several orders of magnitude. As trysting places, they shouldn't be seriously considered.

soon settle in on a few favourites. Remember, however, that it's important for you to look at your particular situation to decide whether it is a less telling behaviour to create a routine and become creatures of habit or to vary your places and hours.

On a final note, let's discuss some of the other, oft-mentioned venues. We've all heard stories of people who have had sex in aeroplane restrooms, lifts, opera boxes, dressing rooms of upscale department stores (why doesn't anybody brag about getting it on in a Tesco?) and the like. I'm sure that some people have actually done it and got an extra thrill out of the danger. I guess it's a matter of personal taste but, since the opportunity to be with your lover is rare and to be savoured, most of the time you will find that you prefer a more leisurely, 'quality' experience.[13] For each couple, the tastes and needs will be a little bit different. A secluded section of an otherwise safe public park or beach may satisfy your thirst for a *little* danger, but, let's face it, aren't you taking enough risks already? Have fun, of course, but, good grief! Use a little judgement!

---

13 I do remember being caught between laughter and terror once when I had received a call in my hotel suite from my boss and we got involved in a long conversation; through the open door, I could hear my lover in the next room, giggling as she sprayed the contents of a can of whipped cream into fanciful designs around critical parts of her anatomy.

SECTION E

Building, Strengthening
and Celebrating Your Extramarital
Relationship

CHAPTER 17

Sharing Common Priorities for Your Affair

By now, you and your lover are probably both feeling that you're in pretty deep. It's exciting all right, but scary, too. What happens in your affair may well depend on which of the affairs described in Chapter 3 it is, and whether you and your affair partner agree in that assessment. Another consideration: are you a graduate (or a refugee, depending on your point of view) of a casual flirtation that exploded into all-out passion despite your best efforts, as in the Introduction of Section A, or someone who carefully and successfully developed a liaison as described in Chapter 9? If you fall into the first, rather than the second, category, this chapter will probably have far greater importance to you. Why? Because the issues which will begin to arise and be discussed here should have already been considered to some extent by the person who has planned for an affair before it began and made choices accordingly.

Big Question Number One (and they don't get any bigger than this): If you could do it today, would you want to divorce your spouse and marry your lover?

If your answer is 'yes', what prevents you from acting on your wish? Or, to be blunt, what's your excuse for not getting a lawyer and getting on with it?

Is your excuse really just another way of answering 'no' to Big Question Number One?

Big Question Number Two (and the corollary to Big Question Number One): Does your lover want to immediately marry *you*?

If you and your lover are not both in the same place with respect to Big Questions Number One and Two, you will need to start talking *now* about establishing ground rules that will either let your affair continue without rancour, recrimination, masochism and martyrdom or planning a winding-down and out strategy that will hurt both parties as little as possible. It will not be easy:

Charles F., 52, married with grown-up children: *I have had a successful affair for ten years and counting. Yes, my lover and I agreed to not hurt more people and she and I are the only ones feeling the pain. I have tried to get her to run off with me, but she refused and I understand why; I guess I am more selfish. I feel that we should do it - get the pain over with and start making a new life together. My lover is older than I am so I have this horrible feeling that I am just running out of time; I am never going to wake up beside someone who loves me. That makes me sad, but it would do me no good to talk my lover into being with me and causing people we love a lot of pain (even though we are not __in__ love with our spouses), because I know this would hurt her, too.*

If you will be relying on the answer to the question 'Am I really, truly in love with my lover?' to decide how to answer Big Question Number One, you will need a reality test: How to Know When You Really Love Someone and When You Don't.

You are going to be making a lot of life-altering decisions based upon the simple question: 'Am I really in love?' Poets, scientists, philosophers and theologians have pondered and debated the simple question 'What is Love?' for millennia. Their discussions will be of absolutely no use to you; what you need is a simple, straightforward, useful definition that you can apply to your own circumstances and help guide you through the maze of hard choices and situations which will confront you.

Years ago, I was at a cocktail party and the conversation of the group had turned ugly. Reports had come out in the news that day about atrocities committed in some third world country and there had been many stories of prisoner torture. The party guests began to discuss, just theoretically, of course, what the most painful torture in the world might be. I had already decided that, if history has shown us anything, it is that mankind's capacity for cruelty has no discernible limits. I found myself overcome with the desire to bring the group's descent into sadomasochism to a halt, even if it meant seeming a bit strange. 'That's easy,' I said, 'and it doesn't even hurt.' I then gave my answer: 'Being forced to watch and hear your own child receive whatever crap you've just been talking about.' There was a shamed silence and the group dispersed.

Obviously there is a point behind this little anecdote. We *know* we love our children; we love them in a way we love no one else. We feel their loss with an intensity that is unrivalled. Their pain and their joys are ours. But how do we know this? We know it because we apply a simple measure and it is one that you can apply to your marriage, your affair and even your faith. Here it is:

You truly love someone if, when balanced directly against each other, their happiness is more important to you than your own.

There's a sweet fairy tale of a movie called *The Princess Bride* whose story is propelled forward by the simple idea that true love is all that matters. How does the hero express his true love for the princess? It is in his simple response to every request she makes upon him: 'As you wish.' Now, obviously, you cannot weigh a trivial desire of your beloved with a tremendous sacrifice of your own: just because my paramour might think it would be nice to own Picasso's *Three Musicians* doesn't mean that I'm going to attempt a robbery of the New York Museum of Modern Art. But if, when taken in the sum of circumstances, you feel that way (even if, for practical reasons, it's unwise to act it out), you are in love; if you don't, you aren't. You may be in lust, desire, infatuation, curiosity, excitement, gratitude, admiration, thrall or something else. You don't have to be terribly wise and introspective to make this judgement, just honest enough with yourself at the critical moments when it's necessary to know.

Jeff and Marlene are typical of what often happens in an affair. They are two marketing executives from different divisions of a large retailer who met when the corporate headquarters sponsored a retreat to rethink the company's overall positioning strategy. Both were married. As their affair progressed over several years, it was obvious to Jeff that Marlene was the woman he felt he had been waiting for all his life. He was ready to tell his wife that their marriage was over and pay whatever price was necessary, both with respect to his personal finances and his career, to spend the rest of his life with Marlene. Marlene, for her part, was terribly torn. She wasn't absolutely sure that she was ready to leave her decent, but boring, husband of ten years, even though Jeff was constantly in her thoughts and she often had elaborate fantasies about how their life together could be.

Their solution, however, was not typical: Jeff knew that the strain on Marlene was not good for either of them. He did not give her a 'him or me' ultimatum to 'help' her. Rather, he said that he understood and respected her conflict. But just going along with their affair, year after year, with the possibility of discovery and all of its fallout looming ever more likely, would not resolve the issue. At Jeff's urging, Marlene found a therapist with whom she set out concrete goals for herself; the most important goal was to find out her true feelings so that, within the next eight months she could reach a decision as to whether to stay with her husband, leave him for Jeff or seek some third alternative involving neither of them. For his part, Jeff said that he would never ask her what was happening in her therapy or if she were any closer to a decision and which way did it look like it was going. He also promised that he would abide by it and not try to change her mind or make her feel bad in any way if her decision was to stay with her husband. Her happiness was paramount to him. Their affair would, if she chose not to leave her husband, be over, because the status quo was preventing them from getting on with their lives. For Jeff, that was the hardest of the promises to make. True to her word, Marlene did reach a decision, although she told Jeff that she needed a three-month extension. Their affair ended. Jeff hurt deeply for many months, but kept his word, even when Marlene indicated that she might want to pick up on the relationship again. Ultimately, Jeff and his wife split up and Marlene went on to have a child with her husband; but it was not until almost two years after the affair with Jeff ended that she finally decided to stop using birth control.

There's no great moral here, just a demonstration of the principle discussed above and what happens when lovers' priorities change or diverge. In this case, Jeff was, for our purposes, truly in love with Marlene but, thanks to her therapy and somewhat to her surprise, Marlene discovered that she was not in love with Jeff.

Obviously, it is nearly impossible to make rational assessments of priorities when in the throes of a love affair's early stages. Emotions, often conflicting, cascade over the lovers, drenching them with both exhilaration and anxiety, confidence and fear. And, of course, neither one wants to appear 'less romantic' by raising practical or logistical questions, but as we discussed in Chapter 10, 'Rules first, mush second.' This also applies to setting out priorities. Let's say then that you are in agreement about the Big Questions and are ready to go forward. A love affair involves candour and sharing. You are in, after all, the time of your life. What should be the common priorities? Here are a few to consider:

1. To give each other only happiness and laughter
2. To find no fault and hold no grudges
3. To make no demands, accepting gladly what the other has to give
4. To be generous with your entire being – mind, body and soul
5. To willingly accept uncertainty and disappointment as part of your circumstances.

Notice that *these* priorities are about how you and your lover are to treat each other.

Other priorities may be: keeping frequency of assignations below a certain level to avoid suspicion, helping one or the other lover weather a crisis or prepare for some event or trial, fulfilling unmet sexual desires, career, personal or academic mentoring, etc.

You and your lover should be talking, from time to time, about your needs from each other, as well as daydreaming about alternative lives. You will feel even closer and will take much joy, courage and comfort from your liaison.

CHAPTER 18

Finding and Being Your Best Self

Did you notice something about the suggested priorities in the previous chapter? They say something about the kind of person you should be striving to be. Obviously in most relationships, at work and at home, we have responsibilities to and expectations of other people to behave in a particular and reliable way. Society could not work without them. But how many times do we find ourselves annoyed at things which don't really matter? Quite often. And why are we so annoyed? Because there is a little voice inside us that is saying, 'Since they didn't care about fulfilling their obligations to me, they don't care about me or respect me. That is insulting, especially since I try so hard to do right by them. Therefore, they love me less than I love them and, therefore, I am hurt and angry.' Whew! What a lot of baggage!

With your lover, you are far more understanding because you

recognise that your relationship has particular risks. Truth is, *every* relationship does to one degree or another. The beauty of a love affair is that it will help you take in the attitudes that you hold about life and yourself from the affair *and spread them to the other parts of your world*: *y*ou will become more caring, accepting and ungrudgingly giving when you start applying your love affair's standards to other people. That's why 'everybody loves a lover'. Their happy attitude towards life is infectious.

> Greta, 34, married fourteen years, in her third year of her affair: *I'm greatly enjoying my special relationship and it certainly hasn't adversely affected the rest of my life, that's for sure. I've got two promotions at work and just seem to have so much more energy. I know, at the beginning, all affairs are about feeling good, being together, sharing and sex; but what if this feeling never ends? I can't imagine my life without him in it.*

We'll talk in Chapters 20 and 21 how this attitude will help you at home with your spouse and children and how your affair may actually *benefit* your family.

In the meantime, you have a chance to learn a little bit more about yourself. What kind of person are you in the presence of your lover? With your lover, are you more capable of compassion, respect for differences of opinion and listening to others rather than just waiting for them to stop talking? Really? That's great. If, on the other hand, you find yourself using this valuable time to rant and rave about your spouse, your boss or generally find fault with others, STOP. You aren't working towards the shared priorities that you and your lover should have and you will soon find your relationship under the same strains as the other areas of your life. The ability to share love is a *precious* gift. It is one of life's greatest joys. To squander it by making it a forum for your other difficulties, not genuinely requiring the empathy and support of your lover, is downright shameful.

OK, let's move on. Is your voice quieter or louder, faster or slower than usual? Are you more courteous or more vulgar? You should list the characteristics that you display and see if they are your usual behaviour or different; mostly worse or (as I'd bet) mostly better. This is the kind of person that you have had within you all along.

Betty, 47, married 23 years: *I lived in a loveless marriage for 20 years and found that I had to beg my husband for a hug. My husband would not shower for a week and, when he did, I knew what that meant. In his eyes, the only thing that mattered was that he was pleased. I began to hate just the mention of sex, then I met this friend of ours who was married and one thing led to another and we had an affair. I promised that I would ask nothing of him and expect nothing from him, but he gave me so much. He gave me back my self-esteem, my life, and made me realise that I don't hate sex. For the first time in my life I had someone that wanted to please only me and now it is a two-way street. We are both still married; no one knows and no one ever will. Our deep-rooted friendship means more to me than just falling into bed. I would give that up in a second rather than lose the friendship of this person.*

What should you do with these new insights? Easy and, thanks to your romance's effect of giving you a new shot of endorphins, almost automatic. Start integrating them into the rest of your life, beginning in venues other than work, family and friends (in a toned-down fashion, of course; after all, we don't want to start off sprinkling 'tells' around). See what kind of reaction you get. You may be surprised at how quickly the world begins to return your sunny gaze and how your performance in seemingly unconnected areas of your life begins to improve.

CHAPTER 19

The Urge to Show Gratitude Materially: The Complexities of Giving Gifts

When we think of extramarital affairs and gift-giving, a cliché from the black-and-white-movies of more than fifty years ago comes to mind:

A middle-aged or older man, dressed in a tuxedo, stands outside the door of a chorus girls' dressing room, a bouquet of flowers in one hand and a jewellery case in the other, waiting for his impoverished but cute little chorine to appear. She finally emerges, kisses her sugar daddy demurely on the cheek, gushes over the jewellery and flowers, and, the morning after, is soon depressed and whining to her friends about the long odds against her ever becoming Mrs Sugar Daddy.

How times change! One of the hallmarks of modern romance is that, most often, it is a relationship of equals, socially, materially and intellectually. Affection is not being bartered and gift-giving is a mutual activity, even if the gifts are not always of precisely equal value.

Les is an orthopaedist in Silicon Valley in the US. *He met Nancy, a software executive, when she brought her 11 year old son into the A&E after he had broken his wrist while skateboarding. Nancy is typical of those who had been able to plushly feather their nests with the stock received before their companies had gone public. She still led one of the design teams, but, thanks to her home computer work station and high-speed digital data link, was able to telecommute at least three days a week. With their flexible hours, they had no trouble seeing each other. When Nancy's biro (the kind she had been using at work for years) ran out of ink while she and Les were together, he made a joke and a mental note – and surprised her at their next assignation with a Mont Blanc roller ball. Nancy was not to be outdone: she hadn't cared much for Les' knock-off watch that he'd bought from a street vendor in San Francisco the year before he'd met her, so she got him 'The Real McCoy' – a solid-gold Rolex President. He was happily stunned.*

Given their circumstances, these were both good gift choices. Why? Several reasons which are worth looking at, even for us poorer mortals. They also serve as guidelines or rules for all affair gift-giving.

Rule Number 1: *The value of the gift must not be so great as to have a material impact on the financial well-being of those for whom the giver is financially responsible.*

In earlier chapters, we discussed the love nestegg and its two-fold purpose. First was to provide you with a source of funds that would be undetected by your spouse and thus not give rise to a 'tell', and, secondly, to insure that your happiness could not be seen as having been gained at the financial expense of your spouse and/or children. This will be particularly important if, at some later date, you are involved in discovery during divorce proceedings and you are required to disclose all gifts and expenses in relation to your affair. Although, in many jurisdictions, those numbers will only be used to calculate what is considered to be part of your share in any settlement, it cannot but help to sway the judge if the gifts and entertainment lavished upon your lover are so far out of line with your circumstances that they could be construed as having wasted joint or spousal assets. In such circumstances, a court could make you pay dearly, 'no-fault' jurisdiction notwithstanding. Les was pulling in around $350,000/year and Nancy's options had brought her net worth to over $13 million. Although lavish for most of us, for them, the gifts were appropriately modest. A general rule of thumb, if one is needed: limit gifts to an annual rate of one percent of your family's gross income, regardless of the size of your love nestegg.

Rule Number 2: *The gift must not 'tell' on its recipient.*
Les's gift to Nancy would be perceived as a 'small change' purchase by anyone who knew her, and Nancy's opulent gift to Les wasn't a tell because he already had a virtually identical watch.

There's no need to repeat what was mentioned earlier about telltale flower petals on car floors or greeting cards with provocative messages. But this is probably an appropriate place to talk about the purpose of gift-giving generally. Often it is to express love or gratitude for a particular act, gesture or statement, but, most commonly, it is to provide your lover with a tangible souvenir: be it of a special day or just your love, admiration and respect for each other. That being the case, the following suggestions are offered as a way to buy each other gifts without incurring undue suspicion.

Want to be cute? Find matching 'his-and-hers' items which, by themselves carry no tell but can carry special, secret emotional ties to your lover. And they can run the gamut from watches (which almost always come in men's and women's versions) to leather goods (matching wallets, gloves, umbrellas, etc.) even down to running shoes. A good method is to purchase these items in two cash transactions and then each lover keeps the corresponding receipt. In the event your spouse notices it, you can always claim you bought it and ask if they like it, offering to return it – maybe – if they don't. Don't try matching with large items of clothing, like shirts with a particularly unique or eye-catching design: if you show up in the same place, the 'Twins' look will surely grab people's attention. And remember, just like other souvenirs, his-and-hers items don't have to be extravagantly priced to reflect extravagant emotions; one of the great things about buying knock-offs is that they convey the message 'Someday, when we can finally be together, we'll have authentic, matching items.'

The last thing you want to do is to give your lover an item that could harm him or her, their marriage or their ability to continue the relationship. The most common example is, of course, sexy underwear. Won't tip off the spouse? Helloo-oo?

Giving clothing or other personal items, whose type or style is out of the ordinary purchase pattern, is always a risk. Male gift-givers have an edge in this department, however, because men are generally less sensitive to changes in their wife's wardrobe that they do not perceive as intimate, if only because women's styles change so much more quickly than men's.

Gillian is a blonde, brown-eyed accountant who wears tailored suits in her conservative office, usually with a pearl necklace or lapel brooch and small gold earrings. One day, while choosing some Hermès ties for himself, a scarf caught Barry's attention because the design seemed to match the colour of Gillian's hair and eyes exactly. He started giving her the scarves, thinking that they would remind her of his ties (and him) and, at the same time, add a little zest to her outfits. She was a bit put off, at first; she had never worn scarves as an accessory, but gave it a try to please Barry and got 'hooked on the look'. It soon became a regular part of her wardrobe. Her spouse was, of course, clueless.

Is it possible to buy your lover something more intimate without increasing the risks of discovery? What you *can* do is window-shop together and then, when you've chosen something, buy it yourself or arrange for your spouse to buy it with you. Cologne is a perfect example of an emotionally loaded product in this category.

You (at unisex fragrance counter): [sniff] 'Hey, Hon, whaddaya think of this?'

Spouse: 'I dunno. Smells OK, I guess.'

You (putting some on and moving closer to spouse in a way

slightly suggestive of romance): 'You think I should buy it or is it just a waste of money?'

Spouse: 'Like I said, it's OK. Go ahead if you want to.'

If you do buy it, don't put it on right away. Why? The reason you bought the cologne after choosing it with your lover is so that both you and your lover can wear *the same smell*. If your lover has been unsuccessful in pulling off the same subterfuge, you'll want to return the fragrance or keep it unopened until you are both able to wear it regularly to mask each other's smell from your spouses. And it will have a second, powerful purpose: every time you put it on or smell it, you will be reminded of your lover.

Obviously, whether you can buy these kinds of items with your spouse is a matter for you alone to gauge. If your spouse comes back with a line like 'Why do you want it? So you can attract someone else?', you can really do no more than put the bottle back on the counter and say frostily, 'Well, excuse me!' Remember, as we discussed in earlier chapters, patience and self-discipline are the key.

Rule Number 3: *The gift should be appropriate to evoke or express the feelings of both lovers.*

Obviously, you shouldn't give a gift that will cause your lover to become uneasy or embarrassed. An affair has subtle components unlike the friendships you have with others, even though those friendships may be very close or life-long. You can giggle about your own and, occasionally, each other's foibles, but gag gifts and practical jokes should be *verboten*. Save your sharp-edged wit and sarcasm for the rest of the world.

Rule Number 4: *The gift should fit into an agreed pattern of lover-to-lover behaviour.*

Earlier we discussed the risks of spontaneity versus planning in carrying on your affair. Gifts need not only be thought out for how others might perceive them, but also for how they will impact on the relationship.

When Ken and Arlene began their affair, he was a fairly high-level executive at his company and she was just beginning to get her career in public relations off the ground at a nearby firm. Arlene was concerned that, despite everything she knew about Ken and the way he treated her as an equal, she might feel like a 'kept woman' if he lavished gifts on her. She also felt guilty that, with a family to support which included college-age children, Ken might be diverting money away from his kids. After discussing her feelings with Ken, he didn't try to persuade her to accept expensive gifts; rather, they decided that, each time they went to bed together, they would read a passage from a favourite book that one or the other had brought along and discuss what moved them about it. It became a way of sharing personal treasures and not a penny was spent.

Finally, let us never forget that the greatest gift you and your lover give each other *is* each other: your time, energy, respect, admiration, affection, counsel and support. These are priceless!

SECTION F

Managing Family Relationships and
Responsibilities

CHAPTER 20

Tending Your Spouse:
Being More and Giving More

My lover and I are both professionals, highly respected in our circles. The reasons why we must remain in our marriages are complicated – and too many to even list. Knowing each other the length of time we did before getting intimate assured the other that this was indeed the first – and only – affair for both of us. What keeps us together is our emotional bond; while society – and, yes, God – frowns on this type of relationship while in a committed marriage, I'm still having a hard time understanding why something so wonderful could be a bad thing. We are not letting our families down. Our marriages have not changed in the least because of our relationship; our 'other lives' remain intact. The only difference is that we have this wonderful time with each other – that is an enhancement of our previous existence.

Theresa T., married twenty years, one child

Lovers who are successful at keeping their affairs secret are generally pretty good at 'compartmentalising', i.e. not seeing one aspect of their lives as part of the broader context of living. This is great for a judge, who must decide a case on the facts placed before the bench, but it's pretty difficult for most of us, being untrained in this sort of control, to keep one's emotions and knowledge from sloshing over from one area of our lives to the next. Leslie L. is typical of what happens when – unlike Theresa T., but like most people – an affair is begun without planning and preparation:

> *This affair business is getting to me. I'm not kidding. It makes me tired. I can't keep my lies straight about where I am, and my hubby is going to catch me if I am not more careful. I am so nervous sometimes I am afraid to go to sleep in case I say something or if my husband gets too close to me or picks up a piece of paper. I am so worried I have left some kind of clue in the car or in my purse. Yet, I know that I have tried to be really careful. The problem is that it is such an exciting and overwhelming time, you don't know whether to trust your guts or not.*

Yet, that's the basis of the 'tell' that you've been practising so hard to mask. You should, hopefully, have improved substantially *before* you and your lover began your relationship. Since the two of you share common goals and neither wants to upset the apple cart at home, it is important to try to *slowly* put things on a more even keel with your spouse. So, how do you do this?

Now that you have found your lover, some of those outside

activities that you got involved in for the purposes of your search can probably be scaled back somewhat without interfering with your available time with your paramour or arousing additional questions. Your worries about establishing the foundation and routinising the logistics of your extramarital relationship should also be diminishing, so, believe it or not, your stress level should be going *down*. This will bear fruit on the homefront: you *should* be able to be a better listener to your spouse and increase your level of empathy for his or her problems. Of course you will be thinking of your lover, but you will be able to spend your quieter moments around the house in contemplation of him or her and not need to fill your thoughts with your beloved in every waking moment. Remember, also, that the happier your spouse becomes (assuming that he or she doesn't have major emotional problems) the less suspicious, more complacent and flexible he or she will be.

Be careful, though. Your spouse's complacency shouldn't be yours. Don't slip up. Don't make things too good too fast, even if you've all of a sudden 'rediscovered' your spouse through your affair. (Don't laugh. It does happen!) Go back and reread Chapter 15. Why do all of this? First of all, you may be feeling pangs of guilt for all of the happiness that you and your lover are now enjoying. Guilt is the biggest driver of telling behaviour – that little space inside you that wants to be discovered and punished so that your sins can be washed away. By being a good spouse, you should be able to relieve some of those feelings and make the likelihood of telling behaviour diminish. There is other family work to do, as well, and we'll discuss that next.

CHAPTER 21

Children and Parents

Your spouse and your lover may be the direct participants in your – to use the slightly antique phrase – 'love triangle', but they aren't the only ones who will be affected by your new status. What about your children and (in some cases) your parents?

With respect to your children, you are probably paying them more attention, not because you are feeling guilty, I hope, but because you're in a better place. After all, since your needs are now being met more completely, you should have more to give. Remember the time you set aside for being with your lover? Many is the time you will find that your lover will not be able to make your two schedules dovetail. Use this unfortunate circumstance to your benefit by taking the allotted time and using it to do something out-of-the-ordinary with your kid: a museum or zoo trip, a walk in the park or maybe just an extra hour on the playground (yet another good way to meet people, by the way).

Early on, we mentioned how devastating divorce is on a child. You may even be remaining in your marriage for their sake. But it is also for *your* sake: the non-custodial parent in a divorce is often deeply hurt by the loss of his or her children. Since you *are* staying, try to use this time to talk, really talk, to your child. That means listening, too. Depending on their ages, you can ask them questions to get a sense of where they're at emotionally – what's on their mind. If you haven't been telling them regularly that you love them, start. We discussed some of these issues back in Chapter 7 and now may be a good time to revisit them. Forging stronger bonds through communication with your children is always a good idea for giving them a solid foundation for their future happiness and, as we'll be discussing in the next chapter, it will do *you* a lot of good later on. Any further comment on the subject is really beyond the scope of this book and I'm confident that, if you're interested, you will avail yourself of the significant number of resources around.

Why would your parents be of concern to you at this time? Obviously, everyone's circumstances are different: you *could* have parents who have a very rigid moral code and for whom you have a great deal of respect (and maybe some leftover childhood-based fear of their disapproval) and would not wish them to be disappointed in you. Although we should not live our lives to keep up the opinion that others have of us (since it doesn't make us happy and won't guarantee *their* happiness, either), there may be practical reasons for doing so, for example, if your folks are loaded. Or, perhaps, they live for their grandchildren and would be petrified at the thought that any turn of events could jeopardise their ability to see them on their usual basis. The odds are that you're not giving them enough credit. They've been around a lot longer than you have and have seen a lot more. They have more understanding, compassion and forgiveness than you might believe.

Bill R., 46, married 25 years, two children: *I had always tried to put up a good front to my parents about Jane's and my marriage, because I didn't want to have a failed marriage, like my two older brothers. But I'd been miserable for a long time and, after about 22 years and with the kids ready to go off to college, I got involved with someone. I thought people would look at me as if I were the typical 'mid-life-crisis male idiot'. When Jane found out and asked for a divorce, I dreaded breaking the news to my folks. What a surprise I got. They hugged me and said they had known all along, but kept their mouths shut because they didn't want to interfere. Then they took me out for dinner and champagne at the best restaurant in town. The divorce wasn't pleasant, but I was always grateful to my parents for the support I got at that moment.*

If you haven't let them get to know you as an adult, now is as good a time as any. They already know your flaws; let them learn about your good side, the non-affair aspects of your interior life, etc. Just don't spend a lot of time griping or whining; no one likes to hear that, not even your Mum and Dad.

SECTION G

Accepting the Odds: Preparing for the
Possible with Your Dignity Intact

CHAPTER 22

Putting Your Other Affairs and Relationships in Order

Your life is pretty nice right now. Things at home are functioning well and you and your sweetie are still happily, romantically entwined in a discreet relationship where you're both following the rules.

Even though we don't like to contemplate our mortality, we still buy life insurance and make out a will because we know that, eventually and sometimes without warning, they will be needed. Although a love affair's exposure is not, thankfully, a preordained event, it is important to prepare for it as you would the Grim Reaper. If your spouse does learn of the affair, he or she may even *remind* you of the Grim Reaper.

You need to start reading books on subject matter you either dread or feel is irrelevant: preparing for and winning a contested divorce and relating to your children (if you still have them at home) when a marriage is falling apart. There are lots of really good volumes out there. Just remember that, as with this book, you can't just buy them and keep them casually around the house; they will cause a spouse just as much anxiety. Most of the practical advice these books provide, however, such as closing credit card accounts, removing contents from safe deposit boxes, etc., doesn't come into play until a divorce decision has been made.

However, there are some preliminary steps that should be taken which, if properly handled, will not constitute telling behaviour. The first of these must be done discreetly, of course.

Task 1: Find the best divorce lawyer in town.
I know this sounds terribly nasty. It isn't. Here's why: you may not want your marriage to end just yet; you want to stay connected to your children or fulfil your ethical obligations. You intend to behave in a rational and mature way. Your motives may be, when put in the worst light, somewhat selfish, but they are *not* vindictive or mean-spirited. You are willing to be reasonable and perhaps even generous with your spouse should it come to ending your marriage.

Your spouse will most probably not be in nearly the same frame of mind. As we'll be discussing later on, if confronted with the reality of your affair, rage, self-pity and the desire for revenge will probably cloud their better judgement (assuming that you think they have any). It would be unfortunate for all parties, even your spouse, if he or she were then able to use the best legal talent in town to arm these base emotions with high-velocity weaponry.

If you live in one of the nation's larger cities, tying up the best divorce lawyers will, of course, not be completely possible.

But you can get a good head start. Do your research. Find out which ones are the 'take no prisoners' types as well as those with other desirable attributes. Initial consultations are usually free or a nominal fee.

Task 2: Get closer to and make peace, if necessary, with those people who really matter in your life.

If your affair does blow up in your face, you will want people who matter to you to be supportive. The higher their opinion of you before the event, the higher it will be afterwards. Unless you're a Catholic priest or nun, your boss shouldn't care, so long as you weren't involved with a co-worker or client and your performance on the job hasn't been adversely affected. It's pretty difficult for friends and relatives to think everything was your fault and condemn you when you have been there to lend them a helping hand or listen to their problems. This holds true tenfold with your children, since your spouse may want to enlist them as foot soldiers in a war against you, as discussed in Chapter 7. Be there for them; listen to them; reassure them that no one, not you or your spouse, is perfect or immune from mistakes. Underscore the virtues of kindness, forgiveness and acceptance in their dealings with each other and the outside world. (These, by the way, are good rules to follow whether you are involved in an affair or not. If you have raised children who are truly *kind* people, everything in their lives will fall into better place for them.)

Task 3: Deploy your assets and revise your spending and career plans in a way that will be the most advantageous in a property settlement.

It may be worthwhile to put off or move ahead faster on some purchases, investments or that big push for a promotion or job change that you have been contemplating. You may wish to change your whole life insurance policy to term life insurance so that any equity that has accrued can be used up as an expense to pay for future premiums. You may want to make your children, rather than your spouse, beneficiaries. If your divorce lawyer, accountant or financial adviser is up to snuff, he or she will be able to give you lots of tips on the financial aspects of planning for a divorce. Listen.

Task 4: Find out how your workplace benefit programmes will be affected by divorce.

A spouse may be entitled to half the fair market value of a retirement plan, for example. You might have to come up with a lot of cash now to pay that out. Do you make a voluntary contribution? Can it be redirected to some other programme that will not be so painful to divvy up or that will benefit you more immediately.

Once you have taken care of these unpleasant tasks, you will have the added peace of mind in knowing that you have done right by your lover and yourself and will be prepared to deal in a rational and intelligent manner with whatever uncertainties come your way.

CHAPTER 23

Graceful Good-byes: Knowing When to Say 'When'

There may well come a time when you and your lover no longer share the common goals you had when your relationship began. It may be weeks. It may be decades. Sometimes, it is merely because the relationship 'burns itself out', i.e. the attraction and expectations of the lovers were not rooted in a genuine emotional connection to each other. Quite often, however, one party to the affair wants to change the status of the relationship to one of greater permanence and legitimacy (as Jeff did in Chapter 17, when he told Marlene that he was ready to leave his wife to marry her) or to end the affair because the strain, damage or sacrifice, either personally or to others, has become too great to happily bear to garner the joys of the relationship.

Although it *does* happen, unfortunately it's a pretty rare situation in which both parties calmly and mutually agree to call it quits and sincerely remain good, but non-sexual, friends.

Laurie, 38, married fifteen years: *I went on a business trip and met a man that was attending the same conference. He and I began talking at a social function and we hit it off. He was married, had four kids and stated that he loved his wife very much. The conversation between us flowed and one thing led to another, and I spent the night with him. We both went back to our own cities the next day. I didn't regret it at all; it was the best sex I ever had, and he made me feel like a real woman, something I hadn't felt in a long time in my marriage! I figured I'd never see him again, but I knew I would never ever forget him. Well, he called me at work the very next day! I had decided that I wanted my marriage to work out and told him so. He said that he NEEDED me. Being 3,000 miles away, I didn't see any harm in talking on the phone; he would call me twice a week. He became my best friend; there was nothing I couldn't talk about. After my marriage broke up for other reasons, he subsequently changed jobs to be able to travel to my city. He made it quite clear that he was staying with his wife and loved her, but he also loved me and couldn't let me go. I agreed to this bizarre arrangement because I didn't want a commitment. He wined and dined me whenever he was in town on business. He met all my friends and family. They all knew the situation, but didn't criticise me. We continued like this for eleven years. I eventually met someone locally who I was very interested in pursuing a 'normal' relationship with and I told him so. He knew he had no 'hold' on me – after all, he had his wife to go home to, and he let go. We tried 'just being friends', but he couldn't deal with it. The last time he visited me, we had a very long and poignant talk and said good-bye.*

You and your lover, regardless of who wants to change the status quo, are both going to hurt and it is going to take all of the maturity that you can muster to see it through in a dignified way.

If you are to be the giver of bad news:
What happened? Was it quick or has it been a long time in coming? Sometimes it's a precipitating event. Let's discuss one of the most common.

Did your spouse find out? If so, you may feel that you have no choice now but to either end or freeze the relationship with no promises for the future, while you work on resolving the issues you have at home one way or the other. You will need to focus all of your intellectual and emotional energy on dealing with your domestic crisis and deciding for yourself where your life will be headed. By the way, *how* were you discovered? Did you somehow sabotage yourself to precipitate a crisis by leaving a fatal clue where your spouse could find it or making a verbal slip of the kind you've managed to avoid for so long? If so, you should try to examine why you did it, even though you may not like yourself too much once you've identified your motive.

Perhaps your lover let the cat out of the bag. Although you may feel that it makes it easier for you to blame them, don't do it. You both undertook a high-risk situation and knew that your cover could be blown by one or the other at any time. This is no time for recrimination or punishment. You may regret that it happened, but it's a reality that you must deal with in the most intelligent way possible, and we discuss that in the next chapter.

You may, for whatever reasons related to your affair partner or just the affair itself, have decided that the relationship isn't right for you. If the decision has been a long time coming, I would hope that you have given your lover some inkling so that it would not come out of the blue. When you sit down with them to break the news, they shouldn't be terribly surprised if the two of you have been communicating adequately.

By the way, if you have decided to dump your lover because you met someone who now appeals to you more, you must be honest with yourself, even if it's not a very attractive trait. You are not doing your lover a favour by staying in the relationship half-heartedly. After all, you're already doing that with your spouse! To cheat on the lover with someone new is *really* cowardly; it's better to bite the bullet and end the first relationship before beginning the next. If nothing else will convince you regarding the need for honourable behaviour, look at the havoc that could be created with STD's during the 'overlap' period!

When the time comes, meet in a place that's far from where you two live or work and where you will only have a limited amount of time together. You will have to decide for yourself whether you two should make love one last time before you break the news. (In general, I would recommend that if the 'dumper' is female and 'dumpee' is male, the answer is yes; if dumper is male and dumpee female, the answer is no. Why? If you do go to bed that last time, the dumped man may feel that you wanted to make love 'just once more' while the woman dumpee might feel that she was being used after you no longer cared about her.) Keep the discussion short. Don't discuss the details of your thinking; that will only deteriorate into a debate. You can't argue about the rationality of your feelings with your lover. You just feel them and your lover should be able to accept that. Don't make excuses. Don't find fault. Thank them and praise them for all the good times. Tell them that they will always have a special place reserved in your heart. Don't discuss your plans for the future. Tell them that, although you are willing to be their friend, you will understand if they don't want to talk to you for a while, but know that you are thinking of them. It's OK for either or both of you to cry, but don't discuss that it's happening.

Even if they are angry, when you are about to leave, *ask* for a hug and a kiss good-bye. Let it be their choice. The kiss, of course, should be friendly, not erotic; the hug strong but with hands still.

If you are the recipient of the bad news:
Are you in shock? You shouldn't be if you and your lover have been communicating about your relationship. Affairs are always risky despite the care and devotion which they are given. Go back to Chapter 17 where we discussed finding common goals. Had you and your lover been in the same place about those goals in recent weeks? Probably not. And, remember, true love is caring about your lover's happiness as much as your own; he or she can never be happy by being coerced into accepting a situation that, after much painful deliberation, is not right for

them. Like the song says, 'If you love someone, set them free.'

So, how do you handle the loss? Typically, handling loss means going through four stages: denial, anger, depression and acceptance. This is no time for revenge, pettiness, martyrdom, the laying on of guilt trips and the like. After all, your lover gave you of him or herself completely and took big risks to be with you. Although it is very hard, be thankful for the memories and the ways in which your life was changed and enriched. If you must dwell on the relationship, dwell on the good things, rather than trying to figure out 'where it went wrong' or bemoaning your sense of loss. This is a good time to comb through your computer, car, drawers, etc. for evidence of your affair (assuming that you've been able to keep it secret) and get rid of it. If some of your mementoes are too cherished to part with, put them away in a packing box, seal it and place it in a secure location. You can even imagine yourself sitting by the fireplace in your dotage, smiling with the joy of recollection as you go through the contents of the box, remembering what a passionate lover you were in your youth!

Keep busy, exercise if you don't already (it will release endorphins and lift your spirits) or increase your level of exercise (more endorphins). Remember, you were loved and cherished in a most intimate way, and, hard as it may be to believe (yes, I know that this was the love of your life), if you want to, you will be again, *and it may even be better.*

If you feel that you may need professional help to deal with it, don't wait for the problem to get really bad. If you need to keep it quiet, use the money from your love nestegg. As an alternative to counselling, a doctor may be willing to prescribe

Prozac, Paxil or some other suitable drug to get you over the hump and back on track. Unless you have also been dealing with other issues in a therapeutic setting, your problem is probably only a temporary one. You will be very vulnerable at this time. So vulnerable that you may even feel the need to confess to your spouse.

DON'T DO IT!

I hope I made myself clear enough. Although it may surprise you, sympathy is just about the last response you will elicit. If, however, you would like to increase your misery and the misery of those around you by several exponents, go ahead. The pain will last far longer than what you will get mourning your lost love. If you need to unburden yourself but don't require or can't afford a therapeutic context, see a member of the clergy, if you're comfortable with that or, as we discussed in Chapter 13, talk with a friend whose profession encompasses the ethical requirement of the keeping of secrets and ask them to apply that standard to your conversations. You *will* be OK.

CHAPTER 24

Dealing with Discovery

*T*he phone rings at your office and you pick it up:
'Hello.'
'Come home immediately.'
'What's up? Are the kids all right?'
'They are, but you're not, you slimy weasel.' Click.
Your mind is racing and you're barely able to keep yourself focused on your job for the rest of the day. It's a good thing you're not working with dangerous machinery. At day's end, zombie-like, you get in your car and dutifully head home to the one place you really don't want to be. How bad is it going to be? Are you in any physical danger? How much does the spouse know? What are you going to say? What are you going to do?

This is probably the chapter you least want to read. It was not fun to write. In an affair, as in any clandestine activity, to be discovered is to fail and to suffer the consequences of that failure. The main issue then is to be prepared for the event so that whatever damage will be done can be minimised, controlled and deflected into the areas where your priorities are lowest.

Getting Through 'The Day': A Step-by-Step Approach

Remember that your highest priority right now should be damage control, i.e. for you *and* your lover. Saving your marriage, if that's what you want and if it's going to be possible, can come later because it certainly can't be worked on now.

Step 1: If it is at all possible, have the confrontation away from the house.

Your home is emotionally loaded. It contains the artifacts of your marriage: your bed, your wedding albums, every possession you ever jointly purchased. Some of these possessions could even end up flying through the air in your general direction. You need to discuss this matter in the context of just being two people. Do not go to a restaurant or other place that is too near to other people. Pick a place to go where you can let your spouse vent: if you are not truly concerned that your spouse may inflict bodily harm upon you, a public park or a remote corner of the car park of a shopping centre where you can get out of the car will do. If you live in an urban area, take a walk.

Step 2: Before admitting or denying anything, try to find out how much they know.

This won't be easy, unless they decide to confront you with the evidence immediately. They may be cagey and try to play a spiteful little cat and mouse game with you. Do your best to keep your temper and answer calmly. Make it plain that you will not answer until they have a handle on their own emotions and can sit quietly and listen. Possible answer: 'You're making big accusations and, true or false, they can bring our marriage down, whether or not that's what you want. Now, what have you got or what have you heard?'

Step 3: Admit to the affair in the least delicate way in order to blunt the desire for details and remove the aura of romance.

It would be truly stupid to begin by saying 'I met this wonderful person and we both felt an immediate attraction. We tried to fight it and just couldn't and finally gave in to our passion.' Don't refer to it as an 'affair'. Much better to say: 'Yeah, we fucked.' That conveys no sense of emotional involvement and any request for details would seem lurid. What can your spouse say next – 'Is that all you did?' – without sounding masochistic or silly.

Step 4: Do a 'Hugh Grant' and make it seem like a crazy aberration.

This is not the time to come completely clean. Save that for your therapy or for a time when heads are cooler and you both have a better sense of where you want your marriage to go. When asked, 'How could you?', say that you don't know even now why you did it, the person wasn't anything special, that you are a complete idiot, that you must have been out of your mind and you'll never do *that* again.

Step 5: Do not blame your spouse even if they offer you the bait.

Your spouse may ask what they did to deserve it or what they did wrong or how they failed you or what the other person had that they didn't. Do not fall into that trap. Do not discuss your marriage and what may have led you to seek someone else. This is no time to criticise them, richly deserve it though they may. Go back and reiterate Step 4.

Step 6: Let them keep talking as long as they don't press for more details.

Your spouse is going to need to rave at you and press you for particulars about your lover. Your answer should be that those kinds of questions make more out of it than it was and that's embarrassing now to even think about them. Don't *ever* reveal the name of your lover. If there was ever an obligation that you signed up for when you began your relationship, this is it. Just say, 'Someone I met. You don't know them.' If they insist on hearing about them, say you *will* tell them , but *not* today. Be firm on that. Always steer the discussion back to yourself and what *you* did. If your spouse insists, then say that the discussion is over for today and, if your spouse wishes, one or the other can stay at a hotel. (Don't offer to go to the hotel because, strange as it may seem, your spouse will think that you are going to meet your lover there!) But close by saying that you understand their anger – you'd be even angrier if you were in their position – and that you would prefer to go home with your spouse if they can handle it. Tell them that they should decide the sleeping arrangements. This will give them a feeling of control in the midst of their helplessness.

Step 7: Insist on not playing out the scene in front of your children.

Your children will have to deal with a lot of confusing feelings to the extent that they are old enough to understand. How well they get through it will depend, in large measure, on whether your spouse has the maturity not to make the children foot soldiers in the battle to fulfil his or her own desires for vindication or revenge. There will be a big difference in your children's emotional health depending on whether your spouse's message is 'Daddy's feelings are hurt' or 'Pray for Mummy tonight, kids, because God is going to make her burn in hell!' There are a number of books that discuss how to deal with these matters and I've listed a few in the Appendix. Assurances of their absence from the scene to protect your children's immediate well-being should be a pre-condition to any conversation. If your spouse says to you, 'You should have thought of that before you started your affair', your answer should be that it is both you and your spouse's job to protect them and nourish their emotional health today and tomorrow, just as you protect and nourish them every other day.

Step 8: If they want to initiate sex, go along with it, carefully.

Strange as it may seem after the big revelation and blowout, there may be an emotional release and your partner may want to have relations with you in an attempt to reforge the bonds he or she now knows to have been torn. *If you are extremely confident that you are not at risk of any physical harm whatsoever*, go ahead as best you can, but be careful; when the foreplay starts, say, 'Promise me you won't mention the subject,' as a precondition for continuing. Don't do any sexual activity that you haven't previously done with your spouse on a regular basis, because it may be that your spouse's reaction will be to assume that it's one of those 'treats' that you only gave to your lover. If they break their promise and start to talk about your affair, get out of bed. You have to mean business at this stage. They'll probably apologise. Give them the best sex you can and say, 'I'm so sorry, sweetheart.' You may even be. But we'll discuss that later.

Facing the Long-term Realities

If we want to forgive someone, we will – however great the transgression or deep the wound. If we don't want to forgive, no apology will be sufficient.
Psychologists' maxim.

You will probably not be able to stay under the same roof with your spouse for long without immediately giving up your lover for good. Only you and your lover will consider this a great and painful loss; it is one for which you will get not one drop of sympathy. Even so, your marriage will probably never be the same. Why? Because, in the majority of cases, even though he or she may want to, your spouse will be unable to and will, in fact, never forget and *never* truly forgive you.

Mark, 50, married ten years to his third wife: *She confessed everything to me from how often they had lunch together to how much better endowed her lover was than I am. Since that time, we have gone on numerous trips to exotic locations, re-kindling our love for one another. I do love her very much, have forgiven her, but can't forget the pain I have and am enduring. My trust in her has all but vanished completely. I am even starting to feel less and less love for her. I have developed a new-found sense of jealousy that I've never experienced before, pushing the redials on the phone to see who she has called, reading the phone bills carefully and calling her mobile phone constantly while she is at work, checking up on her. This is driving both of us crazy. Recently, I've even found myself answering personal ads via the Internet to see if I still have what women want. I haven't pursued anything, but I have been tempted.*

As we mentioned earlier in a similar context, one-third of spouses in this situation choose to divorce the affair-involved partner. Ironically, divorcing the affair partner is often done not because they neither love nor want to live with their spouse, but primarily to save face or extract vengeance (two great and noble motives). Sadly, in the years that follow, the vast majority of those who do divorce the straying partner regret it.

But is this a marriage that *you* will find worthy of staying in? Only you can answer that. The best therapy can usually do is to make the marriage tolerable. Although the authors who have written books on the subject almost always tout the high level of success that *they* have achieved in counselling sessions (see Appendix), those practising therapists with whom I've spoken and who, incidentally, are not trying to supplement their incomes with popular psychology books are not nearly so sanguine: the relationship, in surviving, is transformed into one that is 'realistic' rather than romantic, insofar as the level of trust and the belief in the specialness of the relationship are permanently lost.[14]

But let's say that you sincerely want to salvage your marriage. What can you look forward to in the weeks, months and years after the disclosure of your affair? The books that fit into what I would call the 'Post-affair Therapy Genre' (see Appendix) describe a variety of approaches for dealing with the issues of spousal rage and woundedness. One academic, a person who has become an expert in the subject first hand,[15] states that, for the marriage to *survive* (notice I did not say 'flourish' or 'improve'), the affair-involved spouse must patiently listen to their spouse obsess and rant 'Why?' and 'How could you?', etc. a hundred times a day for months or years and never say 'Can't you get over it?' In most of these books, the authors suggest that, as the straying spouse, you will be expected to do a great deal of the heavy lifting to help your spouse forgive you.

In one form of couples' therapy, you will be regularly reminded that, to save your marriage, you will have to perform the 'Ritual of the Three Rs': 1. claim *responsibility* for everything that happened; 2. regularly *repent* to your spouse for your transgression; and 3. make *restitution* to your spouse for as long as they think they need it. Your spouse may be the one who owns the anger, but it will be your job to let them vent it at you without being able to say anything in your own or, God forbid, your lover's, defence.

14 Their anecdotal data supports a 1988 study by Dr Annette Lawson which found that up to 40% of women and 30% of men said that their confessions did irreparable damage to their marriages.

15 Peggy Vaughan, author of *The Monogamy Myth*, and wife of her fellow Ph.D. who had not one, not two, but sixteen affairs over seven years of their marriage (For you non-maths experts, that's a new girlfriend every five months. I wouldn't dignify that kind of behaviour by calling those liaisons 'affairs'.) Marriage to such a man is not what I would consider a typical experience or one that, Ph.D. or not, I would base any of my conclusions upon.

In another, you will be expected to think negatively of your ex-lover and hold a private 'mock funeral' for him or her (no kidding).

You will not, in return, have every inner burden lifted from you. Why? Because telling everything, positive or negative, about your lover's attributes either at the time of discovery or even under the protective aegis of marriage therapy, will almost always be, for reasons exemplified in Mark's comments, above, a *big* mistake[16] you run a significant risk that the therapy will not be 100% effective and those attributes will be brought up whenever there is any friction between you and your spouse for the rest of your lives and you will be bludgeoned or tormented with it. Heaven help you if, like Mark's wife, you are a woman whose lover had a larger penis than your husband's and you told him so. No matter how irrelevant that may have been, the odds are that it will gnaw at your spouse and he will repay you with a thousandfold miseries. Lie, if necessary. Ditto to the man who tells his wife that his paramour was smart, witty, beautiful, etc. or that the sex he had with his lover was like a revelation of paradise.

Why go through this at all? For the same reasons we discussed in Chapter 7 regarding why you didn't divorce your spouse prior to contemplating an affair. For example, your children will need you now more than ever, if that was your primary motivation. Do your best to help the therapy along, even if it means going through the motions insincerely. (You'll never catch a therapist saying that, but it happens all the time.) But, if those original

---

16 Nevertheless, opinions diverge on this, with many authors opting for disclosure of the intimate, or as the spouse might put it, 'gory' details.

reasons are no longer valid, think again. You don't need to be beaten up because you're feeling guilty and in need of punishment, do you? Because, if you're into that sort of thing, you *do* need therapy, and not necessarily marital.

You may indeed feel that your affair, at least with this particular lover, *was* a mistake and want to preserve your marriage. If, as is not unlikely, therapy does not lead your spouse to forgive you, the preparatory work we recommended in Chapter 22 will have paid off.

There is a final alternative to the acrimonious routes of divorce or therapy, a chancy middle road. Tell your spouse that you are sorry that you had an affair and that it is up to them to decide whether to take you back but, if they do, there is to be no blackmail, no mention of the affair either between you or with anyone else, other than a therapist (who will probably disagree with this tack and insist that you join your spouse in therapy). You will work as hard as you can with him or her on making your marriage better, *but* tell the spouse that it is their responsibility to get rid of their anger, jealousy and sense of betrayal because they are *their* emotions to fix and not yours. They are entitled to one sacrifice from you – a one-time payment to which you will agree if it is not harmful to the marriage, i.e. a large purchase of which you have previously disapproved, a job or residence change, a vacation trip to a place you said you wouldn't visit, etc. Any mention of the affair after that sacrifice has been made will be considered by you to be your spouse's betrayal and you will react accordingly. Get it in writing. By having a written agreement in which you apologise for the affair and in which both parties make new mutual promises, your spouse may feel sufficiently vindicated to help put the matter behind him or her, and, incidentally, so can you. I wish you luck. It will be a necessary ingredient.

Once the tempestuous seas of affair-disclosure-related marital chaos have calmed down to a steel grey, two-foot chop, you can start being a bit more introspective about all of this. Whether you are planning to repair your broken marriage, working towards a divorce or even if you are just continuing your affair in status quo mode, it's time to do some serious introspection. That last stage, and Part III, begin with our next chapter.

PART III
POST-AFFAIR:
YOUR NEXT BIG STEPS

CHAPTER 25

Self-assessment, Part II

Well, where are you now? Or, more importantly, how do you feel about yourself and your life and what are you planning to do to make what remains of it the most useful, fulfilling and worthwhile of experiences?

Back in Chapter 4, you were asked to do a little exercise about listing your priorities and how your spouse and lover could influence them. I hope that you still have the list. *Without looking at it first*, go and do the exercise again with the same level of care that you did it the first time. That's step 1.

Now what? Step 2 is to write down your answers to the following questions:

1. a. Are you still in the midst of your affair? (If you answer 'yes', go on to question 2.)

b. If it's over, did it end as well as it could have?

c. What could *you* have done to improve the outcome?

2. a. Did your spouse learn of the affair? (If you answer 'no', go on to question 3.)

b. If so, was it through confession or discovery?

c. If you confessed your affair, what was your motivation?

d. If you were discovered, to what extent were your actions or those of your lover responsible?

e. Do you regret the confession or discovery? What would you have done differently?

3. What major changes have happened in your life since the time you prepared your first exercise?

a. Your relationship with your spouse: Was it improved or, at least, made more tolerable for you by your affair? Alternatively, did your affair precipitate a crisis or accelerate a meltdown of your relationship?

b. What major changes have occurred in the other important relationships in your life?

4. Assessing the impact of your affair on your life: giving your affair 'credit' or 'blame' for the changes or lack thereof, positive or negative:

a. Separately list those changes which were positive and those which were negative.

b. Weight (not rank) each change by its importance to you.

c. Add the weights of each of the positive changes together and do the same for the negative changes and then

compare these sums to determine whether your affair was
a net positive or negative experience.

Now, let's get out your first exercise and compare the lists.
1. Are your priorities the same? Did needs that once seemed
great now feel unimportant, and vice versa?
2. Does or did your lover fulfil those needs that you expected
your lover would, indeed, satisfy or were you disappointed?
Does or did your lover fulfil some that you hadn't expected
he or she would?
3. Are you deriving more or less pleasure or pain from the other
aspects of your life than you did previously? Are you closer or
further away from achieving the fulfilment of those needs
you felt were most important to you then and most
important to you now?

The changes in your priorities and the level of satisfaction of
your expectations are a pretty good measure of what your affair
is giving or was able to give to you and, on the flip side, it may
also tell you what you sacrificed along the way. Only you can
assess whether it is or was worth it. Once you have a good sense
as to the honest answers to the above questions, you can start to
make some action plans. That's next.

CHAPTER 26

Using What You've Learned

I f you've done a good self-assessment job in the previous chapter, you *should* have at least some idea of what you want to do next. And it may be making a major change in your life.

You and Your Lover: Finally Together?

The first question, of course, is whether or not that future includes your lover. If so, have you and your lover mapped out a future for yourselves, either together or separately? It will be like preparing for a major journey, rather than like planning a wedding. You will have to consider budgeting for the costs (divorces, child support, third household start-up, changes in insurance and miscellaneous benefits, etc.), estimating your timeline to milestone events, developing contingency plans for unexpected mishaps and the like. It may seem a little overwhelming. *It should be.*

Why? Because it is absolutely critical for you at this juncture to look at your circumstances with a cold, unsentimental eye and ask yourself whether your lover is truly the person you would want to marry if you had your choice of every opposite-sex person in the world. Remember early on when we discussed how to go about choosing a lover? The traits you were looking for were not necessarily those that you would want in a spouse. *Now* is the time to revisit this question, even while your heart is sighing 'At Last!!' Even though you may think that now all is rosy, it would be wise to do some premarital counselling (unromantic though it may seem) and a little reading on making second marriages work.

Perhaps you're surprised to realise that all is not going as well between the two of you as it once was. You and your lover always knew that there were risks associated with your relationship and that it was likely to be a temporary arrangement. Did or will you two break up? Whether the break-up happened earlier, as described in Chapter 23, or will happen only after you are both free to make a more public commitment to each other doesn't matter. There will be pain either way and some of the ways to deal with it mentioned back in that chapter will be useful.

Your Spouse and Your Family:
Who's Reconciling with Whom?

Perhaps you've decided that your marriage is worth salvaging. If your affair has ended without having been discovered, you may well have been examining your feelings for some time. We'll get to those thoughts in a bit, but first let's look at the well-known set of circumstances where the cover has been blown. Saving a marriage can't be done unilaterally. Have you and your spouse burned *all* of your bridges yet? You may be able to build new bridges, but they will be different from the ones that came before: the same kind of bridge doesn't exist any more; and, remember, even if cost is no object, some things just aren't *re*buildable. You're going to have to base your future together on a different kind of understanding. If and how you heal your marital relationship is, as we discussed in Chapter 24, the subject of numerous books; I leave it to therapists and therapist/authors to take you through that process either in person or via the printed page. Again, I would refer you to the Appendix which follows the text.

How do you relate to your children once the affair is out in the open? If they are young, they will, obviously, not grasp what has occurred. They will only feel the chaotic emotions with which we are all familiar. A therapeutic setting may well be required to help them deal with the family strain. If your kids are in their mid-teens or older, your task is much easier; any attempts by your spouse to portray you as an unalloyed monster will fail because your children have too strong a grip on reality and sense of themselves and their own capacity to make a judgement to believe it. Here, again, there are many books available to you that deal effectively with this common set of circumstances. I would reiterate a few bits of advice that have served lovers well in these circumstances: *never* justify yourself; it requires you to belittle their other parent. If your older children want to be angry with you and call you names, that's

OK. Do not punish them for their insolence or lack of respect. If they can vent their feelings without retaliation, those feelings will seem less prized. There are a few basic messages that you *do* need to give them, however.

1. I can understand that you are angry and may not want to have a relationship with me right now. In turn, you should not expect me to discuss your parents' marriage with you. No matter how much you may think or feel otherwise, you have not played a role in the quality of our relationship. We own it.

2. If you have any questions about other aspects of your life or the family's life or need me to help you with anything, I will be glad to do so, just as in the past.

3. You don't have to make any deals with me (e.g. socialise nicely with my lover) to get from me what you need.

4. I love you and I always will. When you want to have a relationship with me again, I will be here. I look forward to that day. No matter what you say to me, I will not reject you. (You've got to mean this, by the way, since your children may be apt to parrot some of your spouse's comments. It will sting you to hear someone describe your lover or your extramarital relationship in coarse, mocking or judgemental terms. Don't take them to heart; you're hearing voices of temporary pain.)

You will need to make it plain to your spouse that, regardless of your children's ages, *ad hominem* attacks in statements to the children by either of you are out of bounds. To get that rule established is reason enough, in and of itself, to go to a joint therapy session.

OK. The alternative scenario: your affair is over, but it was never discovered. Should you *still* maintain the secret? What will be 'best' for your marriage? We've been taught in our Judeo-Christian heritage that 'confession is good for the soul'. Some therapists think that only by telling your spouse of your affair can you reduce the odds of future infidelity and establish the 'primacy' of the relationship and that dishonesty can only create distance.[17] In truth, there is no one best way.

'Many unfaithful partners decide to hold on to their secret while they address what's bothering them in the relationship. That's a solution worth considering; you can certainly confront your partner with your unhappiness without revealing the affair or making your partner go through the arduous and delicate task of learning to trust and forgive you... However you decide to handle your secret, the idea that one solution is always better than another is, I believe, an illusion... All you can do is try to make a thoughtful and judicious decision, taking into account both your motives and the impact your behaviour is likely to have on your partner.' [18]

All you should have are your memories (as you ably demonstrated by keeping your affair a secret, you understood that keeping mementoes around is an invitation to disaster). In the previous chapter, you assessed for yourself what you got out of your affair and what you gave up for it, what you learned in the process about your spouse, your family, yourself and the nature of the human relationships. What you do with that knowledge, how you integrate the experience into your life, will, to a large measure, influence your future happiness and the

17 Pittman, Frank, Private Lies, Norton, New York, 1989, P 70.
18 Spring, Ibid at p 258.

values you cherish. If you developed a deeper appreciation for your spouse and your marriage and a commitment to strengthening your relationship, that's great. But, if you are feeling guilty and need to get it out, see a therapist *privately*. To tell your spouse about your infidelity, even years later, will accomplish *nothing* positive. Like the heroine in *The Bridges of Madison County*, the best thing you can do is to carry the secret with you to the grave.

If you learned that there is another, more fulfilling life you can and should be living, your performance of the exercises in this book should have prepared you and helped you to give yourself the strength to carry through your transition with dignity and patience.

CHAPTER 27

Making Your Life's Next Major Commitment

In the course of preparing to write on this subject, I sifted through literally thousands of comments from extramarital lovers, betrayed spouses, lover wannabes, friends, family members and observers. Even though at the beginning of this book I included some quotes from a few people who practically sleepwalked their way into their affairs, I was continually struck by the character of the statements made by the vast majority of those who were the affair-involved partners as opposed to their spouses: those in affairs did not come across as narcissistic, self-indulgent, weak people. Far from it. Most often, they had detailed stories of how hard they had worked in their marriages, how they had struggled to overcome their bitterness at the disappointments with their relationship, how they struggled to balance the often conflicting ethical and moral values with which they had been raised and how desperately they wanted to do the right thing for their spouses, their children and society as a whole, even as they acknowledged the great contribution that their affair was making to their own personal happiness. This book was really for them and those of us like them. It stands alone; that's why it was written.

In contrast, the betrayed spouses came across, in general, as angry, vengeful and self-absorbed. This was the case even where they admitted that the straying spouse had done everything possible to make it right and the affair had ended years before. They seemed to cherish their misery. I was somewhat surprised and more than a little disappointed, but I guess that explains why only 35% of marriages survive an affair's revelation.

From the very beginning, we said that affairs were serious business – joyful and fulfilling, but serious nevertheless because they have far-reaching effects within the lives of the lovers and those around them. By now you should be ready to commit yourself to those things that you've learned from the previous exercises *really matter* to you. You have, hopefully, been able to experience the best and most powerful gifts that a good extramarital affair has to offer and used those gifts to enrich your life and the lives of those around you. If you have been able to integrate the kind of person you have been with your lover into the person you are today, and you are more thoughtful, kind, self-confident and happier because of your affair, you have made the most of your experience. We would also hope that, along with the sweet, secret memories (or the continuing joy of your lover's embrace), you've set yourself on the road to greater personal contentment. Go to it.

APPENDIX

A. Notes to the Text
Preface:

v: Names and minor details have been altered throughout to protect the privacy of those who have been kind enough to share their stories for this book.

Introduction:

Illustration ©1997 by Steve Kelley, San Diego *Union-Tribune*. Used with permission.

Reinisch, June M., PhD., *Kinsey Institute New Report on Sex*, St. Martin's Press, 1991.

A *Time/CNN* poll which came out in August 1998 indicated that women were more forgiving of their women friends who cheat than they were of men, based on the principle that 'they wouldn't have done it unless they were provoked'.

A short note to anxious or suspicious wives:

Italicised quote: Spring, Janice Abrahms, Ph.D., *After the Affair*, HarperCollins, 1996, p. 179. Further: *Ibid.* p. 250.

Chapter 1:

Ninety-seven per cent of mammals do not pairbond, and the female of our closest relative, the chimpanzee, has sex with almost every male in the social group. The males therefore compete for genetic dominance by their sexual stamina. As a result, through the process of natural selection, male chimpanzees have testicles that are very much larger than humans, despite being themselves less than half human size.

According to the 11 August 1997 edition of *The Times* of London, Dr Robert Baker of Manchester University sought to test this theory in humans and conducted a study of 80 male student volunteers, measuring the size of their testicles and surveying their sexual habits. Those men with large testicles were far more likely to be unfaithful to their partners. How would this strategy play out over evolutionary history? These men might not know their children, but they would certainly have had a lot of them. But if this was a successful genetic survival strategy, why are there men with 'average' *cajones*? Dr Baker theorised that it was also a successful male reproductive strategy to stay with the female and nurture the young to maturity. Ladies, get out your calipers!

In the earlier legal tradition, adultery was defined as 'intercourse outside of marriage', and the legal definition of 'intercourse' required penetration. In the ensuing years, a body of law has developed, although not universally, which includes oral sex within the definition of adultery.

Chapter 2:
Italicised quote: Taylor, Richard, *Love Affairs*, Prometheus Books, 1997, p. 69.

Chapter 3:
When informed of President Coolidge's death, US humorist Dorothy Parker responded, 'How could they tell?'

Some of this material is derived from an analysis of the *Kinsey Institute New Report on Sex*, cited earlier, prepared by Wordscapes, Ltd., Calgary, Alberta, Canada.

Chapter 4:
Assisting you through a full-bore self-psychoanalysis is waaaaaaaay beyond the scope of this or probably any other book. It is in the realm of the therapist to aid in such an undertaking. It is, likewise, beyond the scope of this book to help you evaluate the full spectrum of your marital relationship.

To my gentlemen readers: Let's not get silly here, guys. No asking for a Pamela Anderson lookalike who has the investment savvy of Richard Branson and can help you with your golf swing like Tiger Woods.

Chapter 5:
Donald Trump once commented about a supermodel he was dating (what other kind *would* he date): 'I go into a restaurant with her and grown men weep.'

Chapter 7:
Judith Wallerstein's book, *The Unexpected Legacy of Divorce*,

provides a great deal of information on this hot topic of whether it's better for children to have an intact family at the price of parental unhappiness.

Chapter 8:

The issue of invasion of mental privacy can reach an extreme that will ultimately destroy a relationship. A man I know told me once that he had been out shopping at the supermarket with his wife. He picked up a *Cosmo* while waiting in the checkout line and started reading an article titled something like '10 Great Sex Tricks to Thrill Your Man'. His wife snatched the magazine out of his hands and said, 'You're disgusting.' 'What'd I do?' he said. With a perfectly straight face, she replied, 'You're a thought criminal; that's enough.' Needless to say, they're no longer married.

Refusing to be blackmailed about hurting various relatives feelings is not being rude or heartless. It is preventing exploitation. I greatly enjoy being with my grown-up children; they call me often and I get real satisfaction in hearing my twenty-something son and daughter say 'I love you, Dad' when they hang up the phone. I know it's sincere. I would get no pleasure in trying to force them to visit me on some fixed schedule, whether I lived across town or across the country. It is sinful, in my opinion, for parents to blackmail their children with either guilt or threats to visit them.

Banks have a variety of accounts for different customer profiles. Make sure in advance that you can have one which will send information to a P.O. Box. Just having a safe deposit box to keep cash in and take it out as you need it can get awfully cumbersome.

Chapter 15:

E-mail has already replaced love letters and cards for most of us and is a major supplement to telephonic and pager communications. Keeping it from being intercepted is an important task, yet most of us are not adept at encryption.

Chapter 16:

Incidentally, although Bed and Breakfasts probably provide the best ambiance for the money, the owners almost invariably live there and are more concerned about what goes on under their roofs; they're nosier, too, by several orders of magnitude. As trysting places, they shouldn't be seriously considered.

Location isn't the only source of danger. I do remember being caught between laughter and terror once when I had received a call in my hotel suite from my boss and we got involved in a long conversation; through the open door, I could hear my lover in the next room giggling as she sprayed the contents of a can of whipped cream into fanciful designs around critical parts of her anatomy.

Chapter 24:

According to the blurb on her book *Adultery, The Forgivable Sin*, Dr Bonnie Eaker Weil's 'proven methods will increase the odds [of post-affair revelation reconciliation] to a happy 98 percent'.

The anecdotal data from psychotherapists consulted for this book supports a 1988 US study by Dr Annette Lawson which found that up to 40% of women and 30% of men said that their confessions did irreparable damage to their marriages.

That 'first-hand knowledge' academic is Peggy Vaughan,

author of *The Monogamy Myth*, and wife of her fellow PhD who had, not one, not two, but *sixteen* affairs over seven years of their marriage. (For you non-maths experts, that's a new girlfriend every five months! I wouldn't dignify that kind of behaviour by calling those liaisons 'affairs'.) Marriage to such a man is not what I would consider a typical experience or one that, PhD or not, I would base any of *my* conclusions upon.

While my review of the evidence has thoroughly convinced me that no good can come from discussing an affair's particulars with the spouse, opinions diverge on the question of candour, with many authors opting for disclosure of the intimate or, as the spouse might put it, 'gory' details.

Chapter 26:

Comment on re-establishing the primacy of the relationship: Pittman, Frank, *Private Lies*, Norton, New York, 1989, p 70.
Italicised quotation: Spring, *ibid.* p 258.
B. Some Current, Popular Self-Help Books for People Who Have Been Affected by Extramarital Affairs
  Adultery: The Forgivable Sin, Bonnie Eaker Weil, PhD
Affair-Proof Your Marriage: Understanding, Preventing and Surviving an Affair, Lana Staheli
Affairs: A Guide to Working Through the Repercussions of Infidelity, Emily M. Brown
After the Affair: Healing the Pain and Rebuilding Trust When a Partner Has Been Unfaithful, Janis Abrams Spring, PhD
The Extramarital Connection: Sex, Intimacy and Identity, Lynn Atwater
How to Save Your Marriage From an Affair: Seven Steps to

AFFAIR!

Rebuilding a Broken Trust, Dr Ronnie Edell

Infidelity: A Survival Guide, Don-David Lusterman, PhD

Just Between Us Girls: Secrets About Men from the Madam Who Knows, Sydney Biddle Barrows

Men Who Can't Be Faithful, Carol Botwin

The Monogamy Myth: A Personal Handbook for Recovering from Affairs, Peggy Vaughan, PhD

The Myth of the Greener Grass, J. Allan Petersen

Never Satisfied: How and Why Men Cheat, Michael Baisden

The New Other Woman: Contemporary Single Women in Affairs With Married Men, Laurel Walum Richardson

Secret Lovers: Affairs Happen... How to Cope, Luan Linquist

Spying on Your Spouse: A Guide for Anyone Who Suspects a Partner is Cheating, Kelly Squires

Straight Talk About Betrayal, A Self-Help Guide for Couples, Donna R. Bellafiore

Surviving an Affair, Willard F. Harley, Jr., Jennifer Harley

Surviving Betrayal: Hope and Help for Women Whose Partners Have Been Unfaithful: 365 Daily Meditations, Alice May

Surviving Infidelity: Making Decisions, Recovering From the Pain, Rona Subotnik, Gloria Harris

Tempted Women : The Passions, Perils and Agonies of Female Infidelity, Carol Botwin

This Affair is Over!!, Nanette Miner, Sandi Terri